The Blind Spot

in American Public Education

by CLYDE LEMONT HAY

With introduction by HERBERT B. MULFORD

THE MACMILLAN COMPANY
New York: 1950

Acknowledgments

Acknowledgment is made for permission to quote sections from books and magazines to the following:

To The Religious Education Association for an article by Rabbi Morris Adler, an article by J. Paul Williams and an article by Thomas J. Quigley appearing in *Religious Education*.

To *The Christian Advocate* for an article by Herbert E. Erway.

To *The International Journal of Religious Education* for an article by Harrison Elliott, an article by W. W. Sweet and an article by George A. Coe.

To Yale University Press for "Horace Mann and Religion in the Massachusetts Public Schools" by Raymond B. Culver.

To *The Christian Century* for an article by Charles Clayton Morrison and an article by James H. Nichols.

To Charles Scribner's Sons for "Religion in Colonial America" by W. W. Sweet and for "Church and State" by Philip Schaff.

To *The Reader's Digest* for an article by Harry Emerson Fosdick entitled "One World for Religion Too."

To Association Press for "The New Education and Religion" by J. Paul Williams.

To Harper & Brothers for "Public Schools and Spiritual Values" by J. S. Brubacher et al.

For a quotation from "The Life and Writings of Thomas Jefferson" by Samuel E. Forman, copyright 1900, 1927, used by special permission of the publishers, The Bobbs Merrill Company, Inc.

To Longmans, Green & Co., Inc. for "Human Destiny" by Lecomte du Noüy, copyright 1947 by Lecomte du Noüy.

To *The Boston Pilot* for an article by Joseph C. Duggan, "Religious Teaching in the Public School."

To The National Reform Association for "God in Our Public Schools" by W. S. Fleming.

To *The Rotarian Magazine* for an article by J. Edgar Hoover.

To the Bruce Publishing Company for an article by Herbert B. Mulford in *American School Board Journal*.

To the *Phi Delta Kappan* for an excerpt from an article by J. W. Bratton.

To American Council on Education for excerpts by Luther Weigle and F. Ernest Johnson from "Religion and Public Education"; and for quotations from "The Relation of Religion to Public Education, The Basic Principles," Series I, No. 26, A.C.E. Studies, by the Committee on Religion and Education.

Preface

THE THESIS of this book has been a growing conviction with the writer for more than thirty years, an impression which was deepened by over sixteen years spent in the general promotion of Sunday School work. A quarter of a century ago the proposal to introduce any sort of studies in religion into the curriculum of the public schools was taboo with religionists and educationists alike. But particularly during the last decade public opinion has shifted markedly to the support of such a change in public educational policy. It has been one main purpose of this book to chart something of this new trend in educational opinion.

An intensive study of this situation was begun by the writer about four years ago. Since that time the movement of events has been so rapid and kaleidoscopic that four revisions of the original manuscript have been necessary, especially since the United States Supreme Court decision in the Champaign case introduced many new angles into the situation.

I am indebted to many persons for their sympathetic interest in this study. But special acknowledgement is due to Mr. Herbert B. Mulford, widely-known authority on public school board administration, who has been my constant mentor from the very outset of my study and who has written the introduction to this book; also to Mr. J. Edgar Hoover, Director of the Federal Bureau of Investigation, who has been unfailing in his cooperation; to Dr. Charles Clayton Morrison, contributing editor of the *Christian Century*, to Dr. James Alton James, Dean Emeritus of Northwestern University's College of Liberal Arts, and to Dr. Martin H. Bickham, Chairman of the Illinois Inter-racial Commission for their constructive suggestions; to Mr. Robert F. Beach, librarian of Garrett Biblical Institute, and Dr. Preston Bradley, pastor of The People's Church of Chicago, for their critical reviews of the final manuscript; to all those from whose writings quotations have been made; and to Miss Virginia Baker for her stenographic service in preparing the manuscript for publication.

If this book shall in any way serve to create an awareness of the crucial problems facing our American public education, its purpose will have been amply fulfilled.

Clyde Lemont Hay

December 31, 1949

INTRODUCTION *America's Educational Problem*

ONE BASIC, unsolved, and greatly misunderstood educational problem confronts the people of the United States. Stated in question form, it is: What is the reason for and the significance of the widespread religious illiteracy throughout a nation founded on religious principles, whose departments of civil government traditionally follow religious practices, and whose courts persistently have held it to be "a Christian nation"?

The decision of the United States Supreme Court in the famous Champaign, Illinois, "atheist" case on March 8, 1948, has catapulted into the arena of public attention and discussion this problem which for decades has been assuming ever-increasing proportions. That decision, by a vote of eight to one, declared unconstitutional the practices of weekday religious doctrinal training which had been carried on in the Champaign public schools. This mandate of the Supreme Court not only overturned previous Illinois court rulings favorable to the plan and rendered the particular practices unlawful, but also raised many questions about other types of religious education for public school pupils in operation in various parts of the country.

Flowing from this present dilemma are numerous other problems such as:

1. In an epoch of serious break-down in family living, marked by astounding increases in divorces, delinquency, and crime statistics, what is the responsibility of the various agencies to which are farmed out by necessity the moral and spiritual welfare of the nation's children?

2. Have both the religious and secular educational forces of the country signally failed in their respective and overlapping provinces?

3. Is the problem of religious illiteracy ever to be solved by the united efforts of all churches?

4. As presently organized and operated as state-socialized agencies of education, can our public schools of all levels ever hope to offer their pupils a complete and effective education?

5. Are both of these great cultural forces in our national life in default for not having gone, long since, to the heart of this growing national issue to try to divest it of its controversial elements and cooperatively to understand what should be done about the matter?

Some Important Aspects of the Whole Issue

On the international level we are confronted by the obvious clash of two world-shaking ideologies. Our own country, the other democracies of the world, and even vast sections of the population "behind the iron curtain," may be termed religious. Yet Communistic leadership is essentially atheistic. Great groundswells of public opinion flow from these two ideologies. Democracies refuse the idea that the materialistic conception of history, which renounces *all* religious concepts, is something that can satisfy the yearning souls of men who, throughout all historic time, have stumblingly sought to understand God and to discover the purpose and destiny of mankind on earth. Two world wars and the signing of the Atlantic Pact (which Russia and her satellites consider an affront) seem to emphasize the need for religious understanding in establishing moral principles in world affairs. Yet the United Nations seems to dare to do nothing but appease the atheistic sensibilities of those bent upon world disorder and conquest based upon the declaration that "religion is the opiate of the people."

On the national and regional levels, possibly the most immediate problem, aside from combatting Communistic infiltration, is the spectacle of the constant and accelerating increase of divorce, juvenile delinquency, and crime. There are those who contend that there is no direct relationship between moral order and religious faith and practice. Broadly, however, the whole experience of American cultural development contradicts this assumption. It is one thing to disclaim perfection but decidedly a different thing to assume that thousands of years of evolving search for higher and nobler ends through efforts at religious understanding have not basically improved the world in which we live. We see this not only in literature specializing on religion, but in the secular practices of all branches of our governmental agencies where lawmakers, administrators, and courts act on the broad assumption that being steeped in the Hebrew-Christian traditions and beliefs means something in the moral and spiritual life of the nation.

Viewed merely from the historical point of view, our country has a religious background without knowledge of which one can hardly be called a cultured person. The discovery of America and its exploration and settlement were marked by religious activities. The immigrations which gave this country its Anglo-Saxon cast of culture were essentially for the purpose of enjoying freedom of worship. The early colonies not only had "established churches" but, in many cases, were democratic theocracies. The world's first known written democratic constitution came out of the theocratic colony of Connecticut in 1639. Our own Declaration of Independence, our federal and state constitutions, the Northwest Ordinance, and other fundamental laws were written under the impulse of religious convictions. In numerous acts of federal and state administrations positive religious convictions are manifest, evidenced in maintaining religious chapels and chaplains, imprinting postage and coinage with religious connotations, and the like. The courts operate under perjury laws primarily based upon oaths taken on the Bible. The Federal Constitution provides for such an oath for the President, and the latest Presidential inauguration saw the simultaneous use of two Bibles. Most importantly, Congress and the legislatures foster and support religious organizations through tax exemption.

Public education in some measure reflects this history and tradition. Twelve states and Washington, D.C. still require Bible reading in the public schools. More than twice that number permit it. But a number of states draw a sharp line of distinction between the King James version of the Bible and other translations and rule that, because of discrepancies, the Book is sectarian. Therefore it is banned under the policy that no tax money may be expended for sectarian purposes. Notwithstanding such court rulings, thousands of public schools in one way or another recognize religion—chiefly the Christian faith. In keeping with state laws for observing Good Friday, Christmas, Thanksgiving Day, and other special seasons as religious holidays, schools may or may not close. It is common practice to use Christian art, music, and pageantry for Christmas and Easter concerts in schools. Christmas carols are commonly sung and invocations are given at graduation exercises, though sometimes against the protests of certain sects. By and large, many schools are operated to reflect the local majority public opinion concerning religion. Yet so marked is the absence of religious understanding among children and youth of the public schools that a long array of criticisms and challenges stigmatizes state-socialized education as irreligious and as abetting secularization of the entire nation.

The problem of resolving such criticisms and challenges is greatly confused by their number and variety. Possibly the oldest challenge is the very fact of the persistence of (or throwback to) the universal practice in early Christian education, which was to learn to read in order to read the Bible for its moral and religious lessons and for its deeply cultural values. Possibly the most forceful challenge is the mere existence of a multitude of parochial and private schools in which any phase of religion may be taught with impunity. Estimates upon these inroads made on public education are poor. But probably at least 10% of children, on the average, and as high as 33⅓% in larger cities, make use of such schools. A third type of challenge to the tax-supported schools for not solving the problem of national religious understanding comes in a constant outpouring of books and magazine articles, convention utterances, .and the like from hierarchies and individual religious leaders of all faiths. At present there is discerned a tendency on the part of so-called secular educators to accept these challenges, to utter them themselves, and to pose the question of how to solve these problems intelligently.

This last tendency runs afoul of another problem in the shape of the aggressive attitude of so-called secular leaders. On the one hand, they may deny God. On the other hand, they may sanctify democracy to the extent of making its assumptions and practices almost as much a religion as did the Russian Communists when they tried to exalt their materialistic conceptions into the status of a religion. These attitudes are to be found frequently in teachers' colleges, as well as in governmental offices pertaining to public education. One analysis of this situation holds that, whereas heretofore government has striven, through the philosophy of separation of church and state, to be neutral between various religious beliefs, now the tendency is for government to be neutral between *all* religious faiths, on the one hand, and atheistic secularism on the other.

Meanwhile, the numerical development of church membership in the United States tends to put a new face on some of these problems. For some years (since 1936) the national census has not gathered such data. But the *Christian Herald's* latest statistics (1948) put church membership now at the all-time high record of 53% of the population. Yet commentary on these figures, which points to the need of understanding the *quality* as well as the *quantity* aspect of such estimates as of great importance, inferentially serves as another challenge to seek means to break down the secularizing wall of religious illiteracy through some form of popular religious education.

Early in 1949 there were marked demonstrations involving this issue. Prominent newspapers all over the country printed with great display a new story of the life of Jesus Christ. Radio, theater, and much popular literature exploit religious themes. Popular magazines have increasingly been using religious art and commentary which must have at least some small effect in bringing readers to inquisitiveness concerning this national issue. Great national and world-wide efforts at unification of religious forces among Protestant Christians are constantly the subject of news and commentary. Such efforts, however, cannot overlook the fact that the divisiveness of denominational and sectarian splits in organized religion were the basic cause for the enactment of constitutions and laws which, in turn, have been largely responsible for the religious illiteracy of which complaint is made. Whereas in the days of "established churches" of the early states of the Union there were very few denominations, today there are said to be slightly over three hundred religious bodies in the United States. Still, it must be recognized that about 72% of the Protestant church membership of the nation are enrolled within only eleven denominations.

The differences in religious beliefs seem to be the greatest stumbling-block to the rapprochement between professional educational and religious leaders and their movements. The more secularly inclined educationists fear that any sort of approach to real religious understanding through the public schools will so disrupt organization that it may be suicidal. On the other hand, the challenge by religionists is that the structure of public education in general is hollow—that the full personality of the child is not being developed, and that the only way to satisfy parental wishes and childhood needs is further development of parochial and other private schools particularly designed to give what public schools are not now in general giving in any adequate way. Recognizing the danger to public education in such a movement, the International Council of Religious Education has announced its faith in public education and has pleaded with individual Protestant denominations not to confuse or undermine the situation further by adding still other parochial schools.

Numerous current phenomena accentuate the confusion of the issue. Typical are these commonly spoken questions:

1. Why should public schools be at all concerned with matters in the province of the churches?

2. After all, is the problem one of public education, or of religion through the churches?

3. If this situation approximates a national issue, why do not teachers' colleges and universities recognize it as such and prepare teachers to meet it?

Statistics throw some small light on the subject. Nearly half the people of the country have no formal church connections. This suggests that a similar proportion of children and youth have no religious training outside of the meager amount of dubious quality which they pick up accidentally. Thus the churches have no adequate opportunity to reach half the childhood population. As for the effort within the churches, it has been estimated that the average Sunday School pupil receives in a whole year only a fraction as much instruction as he receives every week in secular subjects in the public school. One of the most insistent complaints coming from religious leaders is that the schools monopolize so much of the pupil's time that weekday religious education by the churches confronts at the very start an insurmountable time handicap.

This drives many religious leaders to classify religious orientation among duties already assumed by public education in every other field, such as politics, home economics, art, music, sociology, history, and similar human interests. As previously mentioned, pioneer educationists, who have not been too thoroughly secularized to be sensitive to educational needs and demands, are beginning to accept this challenge and to say that the churches cannot give the needed educational background and that therefore it is a problem of total education, unless we are to admit default and failure.

On the third point, the striking phenomenon of church-established schools, especially those of higher learning, is their own secularization. Their religious efforts are concerned primarily with chapel services, instead of integrating religious orientation with the regular curriculum. Some of the outstanding leaders in colleges and universities are saying that no amount of religious associational work on the fringe of college experience can equal what could be accomplished educationally within the curriculum.

It is striking to note to what degree professional religionists block their own progress by fearing to provide through public school channels a basic understanding of the force created in all human cultures by religion. Denominationalists for the most part, even those avowedly of most liberal leanings, insist upon indoctrination instead of upon a broad and inclusive education, a point of view which is characteristic also of church-fostered schools. Such people seem unable to grasp the meaning of an important finding of a Committee of the American Council on Education which held that great advances could be made if the cultural force of religion were made an informative basis for subsequent training in specific faiths.

It was the fear of sectarian infiltration into our public schools which brought about a series of state and federal court decisions adverse to any church usurpation of public school properties or time schedule. The decision of the United States Supreme Court against the Champaign, Illinois, Board of Education attracted nation-wide commentary, both applauding and sharply differing with the philosophy of the Supreme Court. The stumbling-block in the court cases is basically the failure to understand the difference between religion as a broad, general conception and sectarianism as indoctrination in, or propaganda for, the dogmas of a particular sect. The story is not ended in this phase of the dilemma alone. The so-called Gary Plan, with its 35 years of experience, had reached into more than 3,000 communities, touching some 2,500,000 children with doctrinal teaching. When such practices within public school rooms were banned, those zealous for this particular brand of teaching flocked over to released-time activities *outside* of school buildings, particularly within churches. But this shift is subject to still further litigation.

Where does all this collection of problems leave us? There are several possible steps looking toward an understanding. Over the country there are many minor experiments within public and private schools in the endeavor to establish workable patterns for inculcating religious understanding *within the law*. The focal point in such activities must be well-guided teachers. The American Council on Education touched upon this most important aspect of the whole problem when it pointed out that there are two dangers among teachers—on the one hand, that they might not be even reasonably educated in religion themselves or, on the other hand, that they might be such partisan and sectarian zealots that they would seek unconsciously to indoctrinate in such fashion as to disrupt all otherwise well-planned programs. This situation means definitely that superintendents and administrative councils within given schools must help to guide teachers wisely. But since many such teachers and all new trainees should attend teachers' colleges, it is incumbent upon professors of education to assist in this broad process. As a matter of fact, teacher trainees testify that many professors in such institutions are so secularized that they ridicule the suggestion that this banning of religion from education is a national problem. Such professors of education do their trainees an undoubted harm by not recognizing that, willy nilly, teachers are increasingly confronted with this welter of problems. Training in education which does not recognize *all* the phenomena within the orbit of the profession is questionable training. It may be a long time before the public at large understands the shortcomings within the profession but, as many of the rank and file of public school patrons are finding out, the professional failure to recognize religious illiteracy as caused by a flaw in public education can easily result in greatly discounting the public concern over teacher shortages, inadequate financial support for education, and shortcomings in the physical equipment of the public schools.

There is considerable concern over the detailed content of a body of religious knowledge which can lawfully be taught within the public schools. It is pertinent to inquire whether this concern is not too far in advance of what can sanely come to pass in best educational practices. In the modern school of greatest experience and proficiency the faculty members, guided by the superintendent and curriculum specialists, revise the curriculum with the approval of the school board government, if within the law. An awareness among all teachers of these problems *as problems,* plus considerable knowledge of the force which religion has been in all known cultures, are the preliminaries to any reasonable revisions of the local curriculum. Broadly speaking, the schools are afraid to recognize the national issue as such. Much leadership will be needed to accomplish even a start. Meanwhile, the aloofness of many religious leaders, boards of education, denominational periodicals, and the like, are a powerful block to a public opinion which would make a congenial climate for any open and vigorous attack upon these problems as problems.

Herbert B. Mulford

Wilmette, Illinois
November 11, 1949

Contents

CHAPTER I   *Signs of the Times*

This religious illiteracy manifests itself in two basic ways. First, there is the obvious ignorance of religious history and literature, of doctrine, and forms. The Bible is the "Forgotten Book" of America. The classic characters of Scripture whose names were household words but a generation or two ago are unknown or at least but hazily recalled. The narratives, texts, parables, phrases, and idioms, with which even the unlettered were once familiar, are as an esoteric science to the great body of our contemporaries. . . . The other way in which the absence of religious orientation reveals itself is perhaps even more significant. The chief motivations to conduct and attitude spring, not from religious sources, but from the character of our secular society with its highly emphasized acquisitive and competitive traits; from the world of sport and from the movies, radio, and the popular magazines. . . . Our outstanding statesmen do not speak in the accents of the religious and ethical traditions to which in their private lives they belong. The average citizens, whose thinking constitutes the climate of opinion and sensibility in which their chosen representatives make decisions and formulate policy, manifest no great consciousness of spiritual values. The public press too frequently discusses the great issues of the day without reference to the vital humanitarian principles without which the search for national and international health is sure to fail.

——Rabbi Morris Adler, Congregation Shaary Zedek, Detroit, Michigan, in *Religious Education*, for March–April, 1949.

IN THE introductory chapter attention was called to the present serious break-down in our present-day American home and community life, a situation which perilously threatens our "democratic way of life." Attention was also called to "the clash of two world-shaking ideologies," one of which, the democratic, is based upon Bible principles, and the other of which scorns and defies all authority except that of material might. This conflict of ideologies finds expression on the international as well as on the national level, thus giving rise to all of the vexing problems which are clogging the machinery and obstructing the work of the United Nations. It need occasion no surprise that some of our great universities are being subjected to official government investigation with a view to discovering any subversive tendencies which may there be found in faculty and curricula. It still remains true that as education goes, so goes the life of the nation. America may well look to the foundations upon which its educational structure is being built.

In our own country there are to be seen some ominous surface indications of a serious and deep-seated disorder in our national life which is rapidly undermining the traditions and ideals upon which our nation was founded. As far back as 1929 President Hoover described the crime situation as "the dominant issue before the American people," and then pointed to "a subsidence of our foundations" as the underlying disorder of which crime is but one of the most overt and flagrant surface symptoms.

The Crime Wave

The records of the FBI tell a story which is far from reassuring to those who are concerned for the integrity and security of our national life and who have been looking to our churches and our schools for the purification of our national blood stream. Figures

3

recently received from Mr. J. Edgar Hoover, Director of the Federal Bureau of Investigation, gave the following increases in major crimes for 1948 as compared to the averages for the prewar years of 1938 through 1941:

	Increases
Murder	14.1%
Burglary	16.7%
Robbery	8.9%
Larceny	4.6%
Aggravated assault	68.7%
Rape	49.9%

It will be noted that these increases are for *only a seven-year period* and that most of them outrun our national population increase for the same period. During 1948 fingerprint arrest records received at the FBI totaled 759,698, an increase of 3.5% over the previous all-time high of 1947 which was itself an increase of 13.7% over 1946. Approximately one-tenth of the arrest records received in 1948 represented women and the predominating age of all persons was twenty-one. Fifty-eight percent of all persons arrested had previous fingerprint records on file in Washington. A recent report from Mr. Hoover states that crime in the United States increased 2.7% in cities and 7.6% in rural areas in the first six months of 1949 as compared with the same period of 1948.

War as a Contributing Cause of Crime

But there are still other factors, not classed as crimes, which also reflect the "subsidence of our foundations" to which President Hoover referred. President Harry S. Truman has said, "The aftermath of a world war always includes an increase of juvenile delinquency," a statement which will equally apply also to crimes committed by adults. In trying to account for the present unprecedented crime wave, it should be borne in mind that we are now in the aftermath, not of one world war only, but of *two*, the juvenile delinquents of World War I having become the hardened criminals of the intervening generation and having their criminal contributions augmented by the criminal aftermath of World War II. War is inevitably a school of crime and is always accompanied and followed by a loosening of home and community controls and restraints and by a consequent lessening of regard for law and order. Add to these things the fact that half or more of America's young people, whether in uniform or not, must necessarily have come from that neglected portion of our population who have grown up entirely without any home religious background or church training, and we have all the makings of an era of lawlessness and crime. We are definitely suffering from "a subsidence of our foundations."

Disintegration of the American Home

Furthermore, something has been happening in and to the American home, both by way of break-down and of break-up. Let us remember that the home is the original, most fundamental, and most continuous institution of human society and that it is such by the very nature of its inherent functions. It is the first seat of government, the first school, and the first place of religious training and worship, and furnishes the first experiences in social living. In the course of the development of our modern complex community life, many of the original functions of the home have been more or less "farmed out" to state, municipality, school, church, and other agencies, leaving the home destitute of many of its original functions and controls and with the danger that the surrendered home controls will not fully carry over to community agencies. And it should be remembered that, however home *functions* may be delegated, *original responsibilities* cannot be delegated and thus still inhere in the home. Without a rehabilitation of American home life, there can be no hope for national integrity or security.

Two world wars, together with larger opportunities for women in professional, business, and industrial life, have taken many mothers away from home during the very hours when their presence is most needed in guiding the leisure time and activities of their children. While such employment has often been begun in some national or family emergency, the frequent tendency has been for the employment to be continued after the emergency is over, a situation which is undoubtedly tending to lessen the influence of our homes on the moral life of our rising generation. This disorganized and abnormal home situation has also served to augment the disintegration of the home in still another way.

A government report [1] shows that the divorce rate for that period increased from 1.8 per 1,000 of population in 1936 to 3.6 in 1945, thus doubling the rate in a single decade. Since 1890 the divorce rate has stepped up from one divorce in every 16.2 marriages to one in every 3.2 marriages. The number of divorces increased 238,000 in 1945 as compared to 1940 (war years), while the number of marriages increased only 22,452 for the same period, the increase in divorces thus being more than 10½ times that of the increase in marriages. In the single year of 1945 the number of divorces jumped more than 25% ahead of 1944, the previous all-time high. Records of the federal Office of Vital Statistics on marriage and divorce run back more than sixty years, and in that period the divorce rate per 1,000 of population has risen from 0.5 to 3.6, more than a seven-fold increase. The foregoing facts reveal an increasing centrifugal tendency in our American home life which, if not checked, threatens the integrity of the home as an institution and also of our democratic society.

Liquor as a Crime Stimulant

World War I brought us prohibition as a war measure, a policy which was later embodied in the 18th Amendment to our national Constitution. This Amendment closed 177,000 saloons still remaining in our nation, but the 21st Amendment (repeal)

[1] "Marriage and Divorce in the United States from 1937 to 1945."

opened 436,000 "taverns" in their place,[2] a number which is said to have increased to around 500,000 at the present time. At the time of the enactment of the 18th Amendment, it is said that approximately 95% of the territory of the United States was dry either by local option or state legislation. Repeal, instead of reverting to the situation previous to the 18th Amendment, ruthlessly cast aside all of the previous popular effort in combatting the organized liquor traffic and threw the doors open in every community to just as many dram shops and retail liquor stores as would pay the federal license fee. The 1932 Democratic promise that the saloon should "never, never come back," was fulfilled only by changing the name of the institution and giving it unrestricted liberty within the federal license law.

Since repeal and up through 1945, there was an increase of 3.24 gallons in the average *per capita* consumption of alcoholic beverages in the United States as compared to the pre-prohibition figures. Even this large increase does not include imported wine and beer. This sharp increase in per capita drinking easily accounts for the 226% increase in juvenile drunkenness from 1941 to 1945. The tavern of today is even more deadly than the pre-prohibition saloon, since its appointments are more alluring, since it is found at the country crossroad as well as in the city slum, and since women, as well as men, are welcomed both before and behind the bar. With this deluge of liquor ruthlessly debauching the country, is it any wonder that moral standards have been lowered and that the nation is being inundated by a tidal wave of crime?

That the use of alcoholic beverages is a contributing factor in many major crimes there can be no reason to doubt. The public drinking place has always been a rendezvous where criminals have plotted their evil deeds. A recent letter from Mr. J. Edgar Hoover states that "no research has been conducted by the FBI to determine the relationship between the use of intoxicating

[2] *Christian Herald* statement.

beverages and criminal activities." However, an accompanying bulletin of the FBI reports that, out of 759,698 reported arrests in 1948 for 28 classified types of crime, 181,863 arrests were for drunkenness and 39,584 were for drunken driving. Put together, these two figures represent over 29% of the total reported arrests for 1948. If there were available similar reports from *all* law enforcing agencies, instead of from only a fraction, and if report were made in all arrests of the presence or absence of liquor as a factor, the resultant figures would doubtless arouse the American people to banish forever from our land the licensed manufacture and sale of beverage alcohol. Even in the absence of exact and adequate statistics the uniform testimony of law enforcement officials is to the effect that the use of liquor is one of the most fruitful causes of all types of crime. For instance, Warden Clinton T. Duffy, of San Quentin State Penitentiary, California, says: "Sixty-five percent of those incarcerated in San Quentin are here through their use of alcohol."

The foregoing problems, which are merely the most conspicuous of the many which menace our American life, are but surface symptoms of an underlying and deep-seated disorder which President Herbert Hoover has described as "a subsidence of our foundations," an accelerating trend which neither our churches nor our public schools have been able to abate. In fact, these surface symptoms have come to their worst during the very period when religious agencies have been registering an upward statistical curve.

The latest federal religious statistics are those of 1936. Since that date our only reliable sources of information are the *Christian Herald* and the "Yearbook of American Churches" for church membership, and the International Council of Religious Education for Sunday School enrollments. It is reported that one hundred and fifty years ago the ratio of church members to total population was 1 in 15. In 1948 the *Christian Herald* reported the combined church membership as 53% of the total population.

However, it yet remains to be determined whether the *qualitative* improvement has been commensurate with the quantitative numerical or ratio gains. The only measuring stick for such an estimate is the current moral life of our nation, a picture which is far from encouraging, as the foregoing symptoms indicate.

Furthermore, the upward statistical curves are by no means steady. There have been marked fluctuations of advance and decline which no periodic total can possibly indicate. For the decade of 1870–1879 church membership gains in the United States registered 50% as compared to a total population gain of 30% for the same period. Following that decade the rate of church membership gains, as compared to population gains, steadily declined until for the decade 1930–1939 the 6.1% gain in church membership ran .3% *behind* the population gain of 6.4%. Since 1939 church membership has taken an upward statistical turn. Dr. Samuel McCrea Cavert, of the Federal Council of Churches, states that the annual rate of increase, while behind that of the earlier decades, is yet slightly in advance of population growth. He also points out that 80% of the nation's Protestant church membership is contained within 8 principal denominations, a fact which renders considerably less alarming the divisiveness which the nation's approximately three hundred religious bodies would indicate.

The latest federal census of "Religious Bodies" (1936) reports a total Sunday School pupil enrollment of 18,389,001, a decrease of 2,649,525 as compared to the previous report of 1926. All available statistics mark the period from 1916 to 1940 as an era of sharp fluctuations in Sunday School enrollments. Statistics compiled by the International Council of Religious Education for the years between 1945 and 1948 show a gain of 19,060 Sunday Schools, but a net *loss* of 21,891 pupils, a situation which is far from encouraging. Comparison of the 1947 total enrollment of 24,588,112 with the 40,911,000 population report for the inclusive ages 5–24 leaves a gap of 16,322,888 between our school-age population and our total Sunday School enrollments, a comparison which becomes all the more alarming when we remember that a considerable proportion of the reported Sunday School pupils are *over* twenty-four years of age.

The recent upturns in the curves of church membership and of Sunday School enrollment make all the more ominous the steady and accelerating increases in lawlessness and crime, in the disintegration of the home and of family life, and in the consumption of alcoholic beverages in our nation. If any valid inference is to be derived from the diametrically opposite trends of religious statistics and those of the moral life of our nation, it is that our combined religious forces are at present losing the race for the moral betterment of the nation, with no immediate prospect of changing the direction of the trends or of bringing effective moral and religious training to the estimated 50% or more of our school-age population who are now unreached by any church agencies.

In this situation it seems increasingly imperative that we should expect of our public schools, which theoretically reach *all* of America's boys and girls, that they accept a larger measure of responsibility for the moral and religious training of their pupils than they have hitherto been willing to concede. Lecomte du Noüy is right when he says in his "Human Destiny" that "the courts are filed with youngsters and grown-ups who are not really to blame *because they lack the proper moral training.*" (Italics our own.) If the public schools will accept the challenge of the present situation and on their own motion include moral and religious motivation as an essential part of their total aim, then we may expect that our churches and our schools, working in their separate yet intimately related spheres, will be able to make a much more effective attack on the moral and spiritual problems of the nation and to build again those foundations the "subsidence" of which has brought about the present secularization of our American life.

Herbert E. Erway, Protestant chaplain of Elmira Reformatory, New York, has this to say: [3] "The school has all young Americans a large portion of their youthful lives. Its business is not to teach subject matter but to teach children in the fine art of living. Many parents are ill-equipped to teach morals and ethics; not over 25% of the nation's children are reached seriously by the church; *but the school has all of the children a large share of their time, and it must share the responsibility today for the inclusion of moral and religious ideals.* When the Bible was almost completely ruled out of our public schools, those schools were opened to practical atheism and foreign ideologies. Let us remember that education without character is a liability." (Italics our own.)

[3] *The Christian Advocate,* July 1, 1948.

CHAPTER II *Changed Relations of Religion to Education in America*

Every pupil who enters the public schools has a right to expect, and the public has a right to demand of the teacher, that each pupil shall come out with a more acute sense of right and wrong, higher ideals of life, a more independent and manly character, a higher conception of his duty as a citizen, and a more laudable ambition in life than when he entered. The system ought to be so maintained as to make this certain. The noblest ideals of character are to be found in the Bible. To emulate these is the supreme conception of citizenship. It could not, therefore, have been the intention of the framers of our Constitution to impose the duty upon the Legislature of establishing a system of common schools where morals are to be inculcated and exclude therefrom the lives of the persons who possessed the highest moral attainments.

——Kansas Supreme Court (69 Kan. 53)

OUR AMERICAN institutions have developed under the impulse of three primary urges—religious, political, and economic. Our early seaboard colonization was largely the outgrowth of the persecutions of religious minorities in the lands from which they came and which prompted them to seek a haven in a new land where they would be free to worship God according to the dictates of their own consciences.

The same tyranny which had hampered their religious liberties had likewise expressed itself in political limitations and oppressions which inspired them with the dream of "a government of the people, by the people, and for the people"—one in which the individual would have a full voice in the government under which he would live and where all men would stand in a position of equality before the law.

Along with the aspirations for religious and political liberty was also the desire for economic freedom and opportunity—a condition in which the individual would be given an equitable share of the products of his own genius and industry. However, these three foregoing ambitions could not be achieved without the instrumentality of a fourth basic interest—popular education. Our religion was founded upon the Bible and could not function in the lives of the people unless it could be read and understood; neither could able statesmanship be achieved or effective government be carried on without a literate and informed citizenry; nor could there be the fullest economic opportunity or success without the ability to read, write, and "cipher." Hence, popular education became the "open sesame" to realization of the religious, political, and economic freedoms out of which our nation was to develop. It is with this basic national interest, especially as related to religion, that this present study is concerned.

Religion and education have historically been closely associated in our American life. In fact, through all the Christian centuries religion has ever been the fruitful source and inspiration of popular learning. Christianity was born in an environment of religious legalism which was hostile to it, and the enveloping atmosphere of both Judaism and Christianity was that of the pagan Roman Empire which had lost faith even in its own ancestral gods. In this situation paganism offered the only means of broad intellectual culture, thus presenting a direct challenge to the Christian faith to develop its own culture in schools of its own founding.

The break with classical culture was naturally slow, and it is not surprising that the life of the Christian communities was measurably compromised by its unavoidable contacts with paganism. In fact, it is one of the amazements of history that, under the pressure of its Jewish-pagan environment, Christianity ever survived at all. Nevertheless, by the end of the first century A.D., the new faith had penetrated to the remotest corners of Rome's far-flung empire and within three hundred years had, under Constantine I, become established as the official religion of the Empire.

In the view of the early Christians the monastic life seemed to offer the only safe escape from paganism and came to be regarded as the nearest approach to the ideal which a Christian could make on this earth. Naturally, as this conception gained currency, the value of the classical literature became less and less apparent and, by the time of Gregory the Great (died 604 A.D.), the use of the classics was increasingly discouraged. Likewise, by the same token, a new intellectual culture, based on the teachings of Christianity, was taking shape in the monasteries and was laying the groundwork for new concepts and objectives in education. The ancient Latin language underwent important modifications and became the vehicle for the transmission of Christian ideas. It was the monastery schools which, during the Middle Ages, kept aglow the lamp of learning which, during the Renaissance and the Reformation, burst into a consuming flame. Higher education during the Middle Ages centered in the universities which sprang up under the fosterage of the great cathedrals, while grammar schools and instruction in the monastery schools, in the homes, and by parish priests cared for the lower levels of education.

From the time of the Reformation on, elementary education in the countries of western Europe remained almost wholly in the hands of the churches, which relied on popular learning for the diffusion of Bible knowledge. The invention of printing, the translation of the Bible into the vernacular, and the Protestant Reformation all combined to awaken an interest in education, especially in its elementary phases. The emphasis of the Reformation was on the Bible as the authoritative rule of faith and conduct, the natural result of which was the wide diffusion of education as a means of bringing the Bible within the reach of the masses. Elementary schools sprang up everywhere, almost without exception under the fosterage of the churches.

While the search for religious freedom was the driving motive which brought our forefathers to these shores, it would be a great mistake to infer that the colonists were by any means a unit in the matter of their religious beliefs. On the contrary, each colony had its own separate background of religious history and belief and proceeded to model its institutions accordingly. It would also be erroneous to assume that those who came to the new world to find religious liberty for themselves were very much concerned about similar freedom for those holding divergent religious opinions. As a matter of fact, colonial religious history exhibited narrowness, bigotry, and intolerance scarcely to be surpassed in the annals of free peoples, as may be seen in the episode of the Salem witchcraft. So sure was each sect of the infallible correctness of its own tenets that to accord tolerance to those of differing beliefs would have been considered tantamount to apostasy. Hence, there developed intense rivalry between the different sectarian groups, and religious controversy was the order of the day.

The storm center of religious discussion and dissension was in Massachusetts, where sects were numerous and came into violent conflict with one another. Whereas in 1800 there were represented only 8 separate religious bodies in the state, by 1858 there were 17 and by 1936 (latest federal religious census) there were 56 denominations in Massachusetts reporting three or more churches each, besides 40 unclassified churches scattered through a number of smaller bodies.[1]

The divisive tendency of colonial religion is pointed out by Prof. W. W. Sweet in his "Religion In Colonial America"[2]: "Massachusetts intolerance was one of the principal reasons for the formation of other New England colonies. With the exception of New Haven, all the other New England colonies established after the Massachusetts Bay owe their origin in a greater or less degree to the clash of religion and politics in the Bay colony. Thus, Connecticut's, New Hampshire's, and Rhode Island's beginnings were the direct result of rebellion in Massachusetts, and to a limited degree rebellion contributed to the peopling of the northern shore of Long Island and northern New Jersey."

Especially in view of the religious background of our early colonists, nothing was more natural than that our first schools should follow the pattern which their founders had known overseas. The church was the central institution of the colonial community and the minister was, almost without exception, the best educated person in the parish. To preserve its own life and to perpetuate its own faith, the church felt compelled to educate, and it was common practice for the minister, who had more time as well as more knowledge than anyone else, to be the head teacher and often the only teacher in the school. Not only was

[1] See Appendix on "Sects and Number of Churches in Massachusetts," p. 107.
[2] Page 89.

the school motivated by religious aims, but religion was the principal subject taught. The Bible and the Shorter Catechism were standard curriculum and other textbooks, such as the Horn Books and the New England Primer, were heavily saturated with religion.

So vital were these church schools considered to the welfare of the government, and so closely were they associated with the "town meeting" and other units of government, that they were financed wholly or in part out of public funds. This practice occasioned no debate at the time, since the individual communities were substantially homogeneous in their religious make-up. The local governments considered it their obligation to aid all schools in every possible way, financially as well as otherwise. Later on, when populations became more heterogeneous, as sects multiplied, and especially after the appearance of the tax-supported public school, it became increasingly evident that public financial aid should no longer be continued to sectarian schools. However, state financial aid to church schools was not discontinued in Connecticut until 1818 nor in Massachusetts until 1833.

It was out of this confusion and clash of sectarian belief and organization that our American public-school system developed, and to Massachusetts, which was the hotbed of religious controversy, belongs the honor of giving birth to our system of free tax-supported schools. In 1647 the law was enacted which was not only the foundation of the Massachusetts school system but which was also to become the type of similar legislation throughout the United States. It required that every town of fifty householders establish a school, the master of which should be paid either by the parents of the children or by public tax, as the majority of the town committee might decide. It also provided for a grammar (or preparatory) school in every town of one hundred householders. The significance of this legislation lies in the fact that it foreshadowed the whole system of American tax-supported public instruction, from elementary grades up through secondary, collegiate, and professional schools, covering almost every line of human interest and need. Naturally, the development of the movement was gradual, but it continued until it embraced every stage of human development even up into adulthood which is now receiving an emphasis hitherto unknown.

The year 1776 may be taken as the dividing line between the old educational era and the new. It is in the Declaration of Independence and the Revolutionary War, together with the formation of the new republic and the adoption of the Constitution, that we see the beginning of the shift of interest and emphasis from the churches and their controversies to the new nation and to the new interests and problems connected with it. Statecraft and politics became the all-absorbing foci of public attention, the churches more and more falling into a secondary place of interest.

There is no mention of education either in the Declaration of Independence or in the Constitution, an omission which can be accounted for only on one or the other of two assumptions: (1) that this interest had not yet become a matter of general concern or (2) that the framers of these immortal documents regarded education as fundamentally a matter of local rather than of federal responsibility. Their vital concern for education (and also for religion as a primary element in education) is reflected in the Ordinance of 1787 for the government of the territory north and west of the Ohio River, embracing more than 265,000 square miles. The Ordinance contains this declaration: "Religion, morality, and knowledge being necessary to good government and the happiness of mankind, schools and the means of education shall be forever encouraged," words which would seem to imply that religion and morality were just as much to be taught as were the rudiments of learning.

The educational picture has changed materially since colonial days. Church fosterage of elementary education has practically ceased, except in the case of churches such as the Roman Catholic and Lutheran, where parochial schools are maintained as a matter of sectarian conviction and policy. It yet remains to be seen to what extent, if any, the United States Supreme Court decision in the Champaign case may accelerate the development of church-fostered schools.

Also, the denominational "academies" which were so widespread and popular during the preceding century, have given way to the municipal and township high schools which have become general everywhere, making a connecting link between the elementary schools and college and university. Denominational colleges, universities, and professional schools still continue and are proving valuable contributions to the total educational resources of the nation, though this contribution is not distinctively greater on the moral and religious side than that made by such schools under the administration of the states.

The net result of this gradual shift of educational responsibility from the churches to the state has been to make the state more and more the standardizing agency which shapes the pattern of all education, both as to aim and methods and also, by the same token, to make governmental aims and exigencies dominate in public education and to bring about the gradual disappearance of religion from public education.

Attempts to Bridge the Gap

There have been developed two major religious agencies which it was hoped would help bridge the gap in our total educational enterprise, both of them originating since the beginning of the present century. The first of these is a widespread system of week-day religious education originating in what is known as the "Gary Plan."

About thirty-five years ago, Mr. William Wirt, superintendent of the public schools of Gary, Indiana, challenged the churches of the city with a proposal that, if they would provide the facilities and personnel, he would release pupils from the schools at certain specified periods for religious instruction. Housing facilities were provided by the churches in buildings contiguous to the public schools, a curriculum was developed, and teachers of a high degree of ability were secured to take charge of them, all of this without a cent of expense to the public-school system. A personal inspection of these schools at work showed them to be fully the equal of the public schools in pedagogical efficiency. The work thus auspiciously begun spread rapidly until at a recent date approximately 3,000 communities were carrying on a weekday religious educational program of one type or another, with an estimated enrollment of about 2,500,000 pupils.

In 1948–1949 the Research Division of the National Education Association undertook a survey to discover the present status of the weekday enterprise. Brief questionnaires were sent out to 5,100 local school superintendents in continental United States. The distribution comprised 3,300 cities of over 2,500 population, 1,500 small towns and villages, and 300 counties where an urban community was the core of the county system.

Replies were received from 2,639 school systems, of which 1,621 reported that they had never had a religious education program of any kind; 310 had previously had programs of one type or another but had given them up entirely; and 708 reported that they have some type of program now in operation. Thus, in 1948–1949, 73.2% of the school systems reporting had no program of religious education and only 26.8% report some kind of a program. The 310 systems reporting discontinuance of weekday religious education constituted 11.8% of the total number of systems reporting. A still more significant fact is that 52.3% of these 310 systems gave as the reason of their discontinuance the recent decision of the United States Supreme Court in the McCollum (Champaign) case. These figures may represent a trend from which still further discontinuances may develop, especially if the released-time principle itself should come up for evaluation by the federal Supreme Court, a result which is more than likely to occur.

Just at the moment, the whole status of released-time week-day schools of religion is in an exceedingly uncertain situation which may easily become still more precarious. Information from the office of the International Council of Religious Education states that the released-time principle affects approximately 2,700 weekday schools still operating. The decision in the Champaign case will certainly retard the further progress of the released-time enterprise to offer anything like a satisfactory solution of the problem of religious illiteracy in the United States.

Furthermore, the record of over thirty-five years makes it seem unlikely that the released-time program is in any vital way bridging the chasm between the religiously illiterate portion of our population and those under religious instruction. In the first place, the record shows that 75% of those enrolled in such schools have been duplications of Sunday School enrollments, leaving only 25% of the estimated enrollment of weekday church schools as actual additions to the total number of our population under religious instruction.

In the second place, as a government bulletin [3] states, weekday church schools are not sufficiently well-established to guarantee either continuity or permanence. Being supported entirely by voluntary contributions, they are very sensitive to periods of financial depression. They tend to disappear after their novelty has worn off or when difficulties of finance or of capable teaching personnel begin to appear. The turnover in these schools is so great, the bulletin states, that it is impossible to get comparable statistics from year to year.

In the third place, making full allowance for all that such schools are accomplishing, religious education still remains merely supplemental to the pupil's daily school experience, instead of being an integral part of it. This inevitably leads him to regard religion either as non-essential or, at best, as merely optional.

And, in the fourth place, the released-time weekday church

[3] "Weekday Classes in Religion."

school is adapted mainly to larger communities having a number of churches to share expenses and to insure continuity of administration and of financial support. A recent (1949) report of a study made by the Research Division of the National Education Association shows that, out of 2,639 school systems replying to the questionnaires sent out, 45.9% of cities of over 100,000 responding had religious education programs in operation while, in the five lesser population groups reporting, the percentage of participation steadily decreased until, in the group under 2,500 population, only 17.1% reported such a program in operation. This survey definitely reveals that the vital strength of the released-time movement lies in communities of over 100,000, thus suggesting increasing difficulties in communities of smaller size.

In an article entitled "Are Weekday Schools the Solution?" in the *International Journal of Religious Education* for November, 1940, Harrison S. Elliott says: "The difficulty with weekday religious education is that it introduces another atomistic element into the already broken-up experience of children. Weekday religious education is integrally related neither to their life in the school nor to their life in the church. The experience with weekday religious education during the last thirty-five years has made this evident. . . . Weekday religious education results in the church's not facing its fundamental problem with children, but attempting to solve it by putting them into classes one day a week under public school coercion. . . . Weekday religious education . . . will not solve the problem. It can be solved only by bringing the teaching of religion back into the school and by building up a life for children in church and at home which is educationally sound and definitely Christian."

Daily Vacation Church Schools

A further attempt to bridge the gap between secular education and religious training is the Daily Vacation Church School which originated in the early years of the present century in two independent centers, one in New York under Rev. Robert B. Boville, and the other in Wisconsin under Rev. H. R. Vaughan. The first general organization of the work was set up in 1907, when the National Bible School Committee was formed. Four years later this Committee was incorporated as the Daily Vacation Bible School Association, this in turn being reorganized as the International Association of Daily Vacation Bible Schools. Finally it became a departmental interest of the International Council of Religious Education.

These vacation church schools have made a popular appeal to the American people, coming as they do in the summer when children are free from the demands of the public school and when problems of their leisure time are beginning to multiply. These schools usually open shortly after the close of the public schools and run for a period of from one to several weeks. There is little uniformity of practice with regard either to curriculum or duration of term.

It has been popular to emphasize the obviously constructive values of these schools rather than to point out their inevitable deficiencies. We used to hear it said that a pupil in a daily vacation Bible school received, during its limited term, more hours of actual religious instruction than in a whole year of Sunday School attendance. However, little was said of the inadequate financing of these schools, of the difficulty of sustaining community interest from one summer to the next, of the problem of personnel supply and turnover, of the high rate of mortality of these schools, of the lack of standardization in their conduct, or of the impossibility of carrying the program of one summer over to the next in such a way as to result in anything like continuity in the educational experience of the pupil.

The 1949 report of the International Council of Religious Education lists 54,949 daily vacation church schools, an increase of 23,648 since 1945, and a pupil enrollment of 3,705,238, an increase of 1,648,713 since the 1945 report. But, added to the deficiencies above noted, even this remarkable growth cannot be regarded as making any decisive impact on religious illiteracy in our nation or as offering any satisfactory solution of the religious educational problem. Nor can all of our present religious educational agencies, put together, give any assurance of even an ultimate solution of this basic educational problem of our American communities. Something more must be done if we are to guide any larger portion of our rising generations to a better life. And the only way we can see of reaching *all* the boys and girls of America who are now entirely without any religious orientation is to put back studies into our public schools affording an intelligent understanding of the place which religion has had in history and especially in our own national life.

In an article in *Religious Education* for January–February, 1946, Mr. J. Paul Williams says: "It is clear that today America's churches and synagogues lack sufficient vitality to maintain education which is adequate to provide for the personal religious needs of all the American people. Most of the churches and synagogues do not have enough resources to supply this need for even a majority of their members. But if their schools could build sectarian education on a solid foundation of factual knowledge supplied by the public schools, there would be much more chance that the churches could supply significant educational experiences."

CHAPTER III

The Secularization of American Education

The public school is confessedly and deliberately secular. I am bound, therefore, to lay on the doorstep of our educational system the prime responsibility for the decline of religion and the steady advance of secularism, another name for atheism, in American society. . . . Protestant children in public schools are under an influence with which the churches cannot compete and which they cannot counteract. The public school presents the church with a generation of youth whose minds have been cast in a secular mold. . . . You can educate every child in America in the subjects taught in our public schools and yet our democracy may go down. . . . The last stand of democracy will be in the realm of the people's faith. . . . Democracy is Christianity's gift to the world. And when Christianity fails, democracy fails. The only solution is to open the public schools to include the teachings of religion.

——Excerpts from an address by Charles Clayton Morrison, former editor of *The Christian Century* before 10,000 teachers at Kansas City, Missouri, on November 9, 1940.

In ACCORDANCE with the spirit of the times to put less emphasis on the church and more on the state, it has been inevitable that our public schools should share in the general secularization of the public mind. The period covered by the memory of the writer has been marked by four major developments in the field of education: (1) by the very rapid development and extension of public high schools, the inevitable result of which was the gradual disappearance of the previously existing denominational academies; (2) by the multiplication and expansion of state universities; (3) by the competitive expansion of denominational colleges, universities, and professional schools; and (4) by the growing secularization of these denominational institutions of higher learning under the general trend of the times to model education after the patterns laid down by the state. At one time chapel attendance was compulsory, even in some state universities, but now, even in denominational colleges, the chapel exercise as a religious service is little more than a memory. In state universities where there are denominational religious foundations, students are quite as likely to fall under religious influences as they would if attending denominational schools. As Renwick C. Kennedy, of State Teachers College, Troy, Alabama, says: "Many church-related colleges cannot make as good a show of religious organization as is made by our state college students on a purely voluntary basis."

Legal precedent for the secularization of our public schools was unwittingly made possible by the Massachusetts legislature when, in 1826–1827, it enacted the famous "Massachusetts School Laws," containing this provision: "The school Committee shall never direct to be purchased or used in any of the town schools, any books which are calculated to favor the tenets of any particular sect of Christians." Since the Massachusetts School Laws became the pattern after which the similar legislation of other states was modeled, the above provision in practically the same phrasing has found its way into the school laws of most of our states. But this has been done without any intelligent consideration of the circumstances which gave rise to the original legislation and without taking into account the deep religious conviction which continued to motivate public education in Massachusetts. In that state these laws were designed to save religion from sectarianism; in many other states they have been construed as involving the total exclusion of religion from public education.

Before accepting the Massachusetts statute as proposing or even contemplating the present general exclusion of religion from our tax-supported schools, it will be well to take account of the conditions under which that legislation was passed. We must bear in mind the fact that Massachusetts was the storm center of colonial sectarian controversy and intolerance. We should also take note of the fact that, just before the passage of these laws, still another sect had made its appearance on the Massachusetts stage, a fact which is said to have prompted this part of the school legislation. Even had that not been the case, the wisdom of such a provision was to be amply demonstrated within two decades after the passage of the laws.

No single individual has done more for the development of our American public schools than Horace Mann. When the law of 1827 created the Massachusetts State Board of Education, Mann, a member of the newly appointed Board, was asked to take the office of Secretary, an offer which he accepted. This was a momentous decision to make, for it meant not only stepping aside from a lucrative law practice, but also renouncing all political activities, including his office as President of the Massachusetts Senate.

In his work as Secretary of the Board, Mann strove to follow to the letter the recently enacted school laws of the state, including the stricture against the use of textbooks with a sectarian bias. In the course of his investigations of educational conditions, Mann found many infractions of the law and these he resolutely set about to correct. About a year after his appointment as Secretary, Mann received a letter from the Secretary of the American Sunday School Union asking his approval of the Union's "Select Library" for inclusion in the public-school libraries then being promoted by the State Board of Education. On examining the books in question, Mann found them to be flagrantly sectarian and refused to give them his endorsement. This refusal led to a long campaign of vilification on the part of the Sunday School Union's Secretary in which he even carried the matter to the State School Board and to the Legislature in his endeavor to oust Mann from his position, even using Mann's Unitarian connection as an argument against his fitness for his position. It is to the credit both of the State School Board and of the Legislature that they consistently upheld Mann and his administration until 1848, when he resigned to accept an appointment to the national House of Representatives to fill a vacancy caused by the death of John Quincy Adams.

That it was no part of Mann's purpose to exclude religion, but only sectarian textbooks and teaching, from the schools of Massachusetts, is amply proven by his own statements. In his first report to the State Board of Education, he dealt with the School Laws passed March 10, 1827, and with the infractions of those laws which he had discovered thus early in his administration. After justifying his endeavor to exclude sectarian textbooks from the schools, he added: "Entirely to discard the inculcation of the great doctrines of morality and of natural theology has a vehement tendency to drive mankind into opposite extremes; to make them devotees on one side, or profligates on the other; each about equally regardless of the true constituents of human welfare. Against a tendency to these two fatal extremes the beautiful and sublime truths of ethics and natural religion have a poising power." [1]

In a letter to Rev. Matthew Hale Smith, who accused him of heresy, Mann wrote: "Every one who has availed himself of the means of arriving at the truth on this point, knows that I am in favor of religious instruction in our schools to the extremest verge to which it can be carried without invading those rights of conscience which are established by the laws of God and guaranteed to us by the Constitution of the State." [2]

If any further evidence were required to prove that it was no part of Mann's purpose to eliminate religion from the schools of Massachusetts, it would be found in his final report to the Legislature at the close of his twelve years of service as the Secretary of the State Board of Education and more than twenty years after the passage of the anti-sectarian laws: "Moral education is a primal necessity of social existence. The grand result in practical education can never be attained without religion and no community will ever be religious without religious education. . . . Had the Board required me to exclude either the Bible or religious instruction, I certainly should have given the earliest opportunity to appoint my successor." [3]

Two things are evident: (1) that secularization of our schools did not originate with Horace Mann and (2) that the Massachusetts anti-sectarian laws, after which the similar legislation of most of the other states has been patterned, did not contemplate the exclusion either of the Bible or of religious instruction from the schools of that state, a conclusion still further supported by the fact that daily reading of the Bible in the schools is required by Massachusetts statute even to this day.

According to a well-recognized legal principle, the intent of the

[1] Raymond B. Culver, "Horace Mann and Religion in the Massachusetts Public Schools," page 42.

[2] Raymond B. Culver, "Horace Mann and Religion in the Massachusetts Public Schools," page 297.

[3] Quoted by W. S. Fleming, "God In Our Public Schools," page 29.

makers of a law is the fundamental basis for the interpretation of that law, and hence the original intention of the framers of the Massachusetts School Laws may well be taken into account in interpreting all other legislation modeled after the Massachusetts law. On the above-mentioned legal principle, those closest to the framing of the Massachusetts School Laws of 1826–1827 should be regarded as the ablest and truest interpreters of those laws. During the controversy between Mann and the Secretary of the American Sunday School Union over Mann's library policies, the Committee on that matter reported to the State Board of Education as follows:

While the Legislature requires the children in our common schools to be taught the principles of piety and virtue and prohibits the propagation of sectarian views, it cannot in truth be said that the Legislature or the Board of Education are regardless of the religious instruction of the children and youth of the commonwealth. On the contrary, the facts prove that Massachusetts still retains and cherishes the great principles of freedom that were cherished by her Puritan ancestors. *By her law she enjoins that children shall be taught the principles common to all sects and then wisely leaves it to parents and to the several denominations to complete the system, each according to his own views.* (Italics our own)

July, 1838

E. DAVIS
THOMAS ROBBINS
GEORGE PUTNAM

In all propriety, Mann's own statements and such declarations as that of this Committee should form the basis for interpreting the anti-sectarian school legislation of all those states which modeled their laws after those of Massachusetts.

But what happens to a law after it leaves the hands of the framers and falls into the hands of the interpreters is quite another matter. Other states followed Massachusetts in the enactment of legislation forbidding sectarian teaching and the use of textbooks with a sectarian bias, New Jersey, in 1844, being the first to take such action. Following that date, twenty-one states already in the Union passed such restrictive amendments to their constitutions, and seventeen other states have included such measures on their admission into the Commonwealth of States.

The conclusion of this process of secularizing our public schools is emphasized in the opinion of four concurring Justices in the United States Supreme Court decision in the Champaign weekday religious case on March 8, 1948. These Justices stated: "By 1875 the separation of public education from church entanglements, of the state from the teaching of religion, was firmly established in the consciousness of the nation. . . . The extent to which this principle was deemed a presupposition of our Constitutional system is strikingly illustrated by the fact that every state admitted into the Union since 1876 was compelled by Congress to write into its constitution a requirement that it maintain a school system free from sectarian control." About one-fourth of our present forty-eight states were thus forced by Congress to secularize their educational systems.[4]

It should be noted that the actual language of practically all of these state laws prohibits the teaching, not of religion, but of sectarianism. Thus it would seem that the complete elimination of religion from our public schools was not even contemplated by those who framed and passed the original anti-sectarian laws. No law has ever been passed by any state forbidding the use of the Bible in the public schools, but the exclusion of the Bible in the schools of some of our states has been brought about through interpretations of the law either by the courts or by Attorneys General.

Anticipating for a moment the theme of the next chapter, it should here be said that nowhere in all the vexed controversies in Massachusetts does the present writer recall that the principle of the separation of church and state was ever invoked in justification of the anti-sectarian school laws nor has he known of its having been cited in support of the adoption of such laws by

[4] See Appendix, page 109.

other states. It is evident that this basic American principle was not the *cause* of the adoption of these laws but that, in a later stage, it was invoked in favor of excluding the Bible and religion from our public schools, an extension of meaning which was never intended or even contemplated by the framers of the antisectarian laws or by any provision of our federal Constitution.

That it was not the fault or intent of the originators of these laws that the Bible and religion should be forced out of our schools is further evidenced by the fact that the Bible is still permitted, and in a number of cases even required, to be read in the schools of some states having such restrictions, Massachusetts herself making mandatory the daily reading of the Bible in the schools. Neither was the Bible driven from our schools by popular demand. What happened was that certain minority pressure groups by-passed courts and legislatures and brought enough pressure to bear on local school boards and superintendents to accomplish what never could have been done by more public and direct political action. In an article on "Our Educational Dilemma" in *The International Journal of Religious Education* for November, 1940, Prof. W. W. Sweet says: "In the whole course of the struggle for the separation of church and state in the United States, and everywhere else where it has triumphed, majority groups have uniformly opposed it. Rather it has been achieved by minorities combining their forces with the unchurched and with those who have no strong religious loyalties."

Commenting on the present secularized state of public education, President Nicholas Murray Butler, former head of Columbia University, said in his annual report for 1934: "The separation of church and state is fundamental in American political order, but so far as religious education is concerned, this principle has been so far departed from as to put the whole force and influence of the tax-supported schools on the side of one element in the community—that which is pagan and believes in no religion whatever."

Luther A. Weigle, Dean Emeritus of Yale University Divinity School, says: "A system of public education that gives no place to religion is not in reality neutral, but exerts an influence, unintentional though it is, *against* religion. For the state not to include in its educational program a definite recognition of the place and value of religion in human life is to convey to children, with all the prestige and authority of the school maintained by the state, the suggestion that religion has no real place and value. The omission of religion from the public schools conveys a condemnatory suggestion to the children."

In an article by Charles Clayton Morrison entitled "Protestantism and the Public School," in *The Christian Century* of April 17, 1946, he says: "A way must therefore be found to incorporate the teaching of religion in the public school system as an integral part of the curriculum, in accordance with modern educational theory, if the downward curve of our culture toward religious illiteracy and secularism is to be arrested. Such a way, I believe, can be found. Its difficulty is in large part due to an inherited taboo. If we approach it in the light of modern pedagogical theory and method, and with fresh and open minds, the taboo can be dispelled. . . . The time has come to break the taboo against religion in general education. If the churches are not able to show how this absurd interdiction can be broken, let the teaching profession challenge them by showing how it can be done. One thing is sure, Protestantism cannot long maintain its position in American culture while it continues to allow its children to grow up in religious illiteracy. Catholicism, with its parochial schools, in which not only knowledge about their religion is imparted, but religious devotion is inculcated, is in a position to take advantage of the vacuum in the general culture, and it is acting accordingly. Until Protestantism awakens to the fact that its position is vulnerable to Catholicism on the one hand and to secularism on the other, its hope of winning America is a blind illusion."

CHAPTER IV

Church and State as Related to Public Education

Here in America we believe in the separation of church and state. It is a sound principle, but one that is much misunderstood. It means just what the phrase implies—that church and state are mutually free. It means a separation of control, so that neither church nor state will attempt to control the other. But it does not mean that the state acknowledges no God, or that the state is exempt from the moral law wherewith God sets the bounds of justice for nations as for individuals. . . . The religious faith of America has inspired our history as a people and is embodied in our most characteristic institutions. America has no state church, but the American government is not godless. The American government favors no sect and fosters no sectarianism, but it is founded on faith in God and it protects religion. . . . The public schools should aim at the development of a citizenship which is founded on character; and they may, in their efforts to educate for character, give due place to religious motives. They can teach that morality is more than custom, public opinion, or legal enactment; they can point to its grounding in the structure of the universe and in the nature of God. They can, in the teaching of history, literature, and the social sciences, afford to religious faith its normal and proper place.

——Luther A. Weigle, Dean Emeritus of Yale Divinity School, in "Religion and Public Education," pages 32-34.

THE RELATIONSHIP of organized religion and the state to each other has throughout history been one of continuous discussion, disagreement, and often of open conflict. We find these two institutions, church and state, existing side by side in different and supposedly separate spheres and professedly subject to different sovereignties. These two spheres are theoretically separate but actually, at times, each tends to spill over into the domain of the other. The complicating feature of the situation is that adherents of the church are also at the same time citizens of the state and that the exigencies and demands of the state frequently run counter to the principles and objectives of the church.

The state, as a purely human institution, assumes exclusive jurisdiction over the political interests and allegiances of its subjects and is theoretically responsible for all interests pertaining to their material welfare, including economic phases as well. The church, on the other hand, claims a divine origin and theoretically acknowledges only a divine sovereignty, though this is administered through human agents who are also citizens of the state and owe obligations to it.

It was inevitable that these two sovereignties, church and state, should at times come into conflict, especially when the problems and exigencies of the state became pressingly acute. It may with truth be said that the church-state relationship is the warp upon which the tapestry of history is woven, for there is scarcely a crisis within or between nations in which the conflict of these two jurisdictions does not color the scene. One or the other tends to dominate. Generally the state has overshadowed the church and has succeeded in making its own claims primary, thus leaving the church in the relative position of a vassal. At times, however, the church has grown so powerful as to encroach upon the sovereignty of the state, even to the point of claiming and exercising the right to crown the heads of states. In the Hebrew nation this "balance of power" was settled by the creation of a theocratic state in which the political interest was entirely subordinated to the ecclesiastical, but this theocratic state in time became completely dominated by the strong, outreaching arm of the Roman Empire.

As a rule, the policy of these two conflicting sovereignties has been to get along together as amicably as possible, the church being glad to avail herself of the protection of the state and the state being content to enjoy the sanction, blessing, and aid of the church. But it is easy to see that, in such an alliance of temporal and spiritual interests, moral and spiritual principles would easily become compromised in times of acute crisis for the state. It is obvious that the two sovereignties cannot continuously exist on a plane of absolute parity. In the final analysis, there can be but one supreme sovereignty and, for the Christian, that must ever be the sovereignty of conscience and of the law of God, a situation which must often mean economic and civil hardship or else the yielding of one's religious convictions.

It is out of the inevitable conflict of these two sovereignties that democracy was born. Wherever and whenever men have felt the imperative urgings of conscience, that moment they have felt the impulse to resist the encroachment of any opposing authority, and thus the seeds of revolution were sown. All through the prophetical writings of the Old Testament the supremacy of the individual conscience over the domination of any opposing power is the prevailing note, and upon these writings, which constitute the Magna Carta of democracy, Jesus rested his principle of the supreme importance of the individual. The sovereignty of conscience is the indispensable condition for the growth of democracy.

In the Christian era, church-state relationships have been a vexing problem ever since the time of Constantine I. In making the state Christian, Constantine made of the church an instiution under imperial control, a subordination from which the church has never fully recovered. Sacerdotalism was united with imperialism in the person of the Emperor. The church acquiesced in this arrangement in view of the security and immunities thus gained, but that did not prevent her at times from resisting heretical emperors. The political principle which Constantine had taken for granted was fully recognized under Theodosius I and, notwithstanding protests from time to time, proved permanent. This Christian Roman Empire, from the first Constantine to the last, endured for 1,130 years and, during that long period which witnessed the birth of all the great nations of modern Europe, it experienced many fluctuations of revival and decline.

The fall of this Christian Roman Empire was one of the causes which led up to the Protestant Reformation and made it possible. It culminated in a new alignment of Christian forces, the Roman Catholic Church working steadily to regain her lost temporal power, and Protestants veering more and more to an insistence on the separation of church and state. As a halfway step in that general direction, one of the outcomes of the Reformation was the emergence of national churches in England, in Holland, and in the German and Scandinavian states.

The Reformation embodied separatist principles which also gave rise to all sorts of smaller sects, each of them stressing one or another of the primitive features of Christianity. Almost universally these smaller sects were persecuted by those more firmly established, as well as by the Roman Catholic Church. Naturally, these persecuted sects were clamorous in their demand for religious liberty and it was with them that the insistence arose for a more complete separation of church and state. This movement transferred itself to America where, owing to the influences which affected our early settlement, sects were numerous and sectarian differences and prejudices were rife. Any semblance of union of church with our national government would have been greeted with violent protest by all sects except the one which might seem to profit by such an arrangement. From the standpoint of the state, the only way to avoid internal troubles seemed to be to put all sects on an equal footing before the law, a policy which later was embodied in our federal Constitution. The wisdom of this policy has been amply justified.

The great religious awakenings of the eighteenth century increased the number of dissenting sects and also, through a growing tendency to toleration, multiplied the numbers of the unchurched and indifferent in our population. It is significant that a number of the most important leaders in the fight for religious liberty were non-church members, such as Madison, Jefferson, Franklin, and possibly even Washington himself, whose actual affiliation with the church has been questioned. It was an age of free thinking—scientifically, politically, and religiously. The general tendency of the times to break away from traditional interpretations of religion may be seen in Thomas Paine's "Age of Reason."

In his "Religion In Colonial America," [1] Prof. W. W. Sweet sets forth the views of Roger Williams, of Providence, Rhode Island, in the middle of the seventeenth century, concerning the relations of church and state. The following excerpts from Prof. Sweet's summarization epitomize the policy of the separation of church and state which has become traditional in our nation: "The conception of the church as a part of the state Williams totally rejected on the ground that the two were essentially different. The state's function, whether among Christians or pagans, is to exercise temporal control. The source of civil power is not religious, but natural, and flows from society. He denied the supernatural rights of civil government, thus flatly contradicting the whole Massachusetts contention regarding the divine origin of their magistracy. . . . When religion attempts to interfere in the affairs of the civil state, as in Massachusetts, it weakens and undermines the state's legitimate power—the state becomes the tool of the

[1] Pages 125–126.

church and does not function in its own right. . . . As the state
is supreme in temporal affairs, so religion is supreme in spiritual.
. . . Out of this view of the complete separation of the church
from the state comes naturally the freedom of conscience and of
worship."

It was this view of the distinct and separate character and function of church and state which, a century and a half later than
Williams' time, was to find expression in the United States Constitution in these words: "Congress shall make no law respecting
an establishment of religion or prohibiting the free exercise
thereof." The founders of our government were very wise in thus
steering clear of the difficulties either of the domination of the
state by the church or of the church by the state. To them it
seemed best to make the two entirely independent of each other,
a policy the wisdom of which is becoming increasingly evident
as time goes by.

Dr. Philip Schaff, in his book "Church And State," [2] says, "Religion and liberty are inseparable. Religion is voluntary and cannot
and ought not to be enforced. . . . Such liberty is impossible on
the basis of a union of church and state, where the one restrains
or controls the other. It requires a friendly separation, where
each power is entirely independent in its own sphere. The church,
as such, has nothing to do with the state except to obey its laws
and strengthen its moral foundations: the state has nothing to do
with the church except to protect her in her property and liberty,
and the state must be equally just to all forms of belief and un-
belief which do not endanger the public safety."

The purpose of our founders to make no establishment of religion arose: (1) from their observance of the evils of state-domi-
nated churches in the lands from which they came and (2) from
the lively sectarian controversies which threatened the unity of
government in America, where there developed Puritan, Angli-
can, Huguenot, Dutch, Quaker, Catholic, Mennonite, and other

[2] Pages 9–10.

religious communities, each at first homogeneous in its religious make-up, but tending to come more or less into contact and also into conflict with one another. It is just a bit surprising today to be reminded that the only Roman Catholic colony, that under Lord Baltimore in Maryland, was probably the most tolerant of all.

So evident were the ideals of religious liberty which underlay our national life that the religiously oppressed of other nations naturally came to our shores to find freedom for their faith. Sects multiplied both by immigration and also by division until there are now said to be slightly over three hundred religious bodies in our nation. In such an agglomeration of religious opinions and practices it seems exceedingly wise that no union of church and state should be attempted.

Our Nation Not Intended to Be Irreligious

What, then, was intended to be the place of religion in a nation where church and state were separate? The separation of these two interests was never intended to be construed as an act against religion or to mean that the state should be indifferent to it. What it does mean is that the state as an institution shall never hamper or coerce the church, and that the church as an institution shall never control or intimidate the state. However, there is a vast difference between the church as an institution and religion as a human faith and experience. The church organizes, disciplines its members, draws men into its ministry, amasses property, looks to the state for protection in these property rights, and usually is not slow in asserting these rights. Religion, on the other hand, springs up spontaneously within the human breast and spreads from soul to soul and, theoretically at least, is separate from all those institutional involvements on account of which church and state are forever separate in our nation. If religion could be entirely divorced from institutionalism, there would be much less rooting place for controversy.

That the founders of our government intended that this nation should be Christian in character and declared purpose there cannot be the slightest shadow of a doubt. That this is a Christian nation has been declared again and again by our state and federal courts and by men eminent in the affairs of the nation. In the celebrated Girard Will Case (February, 1844) Daniel Webster said: "There is nothing we look for with more certainty than the general principle that Christianity is part of the law of the land. . . . And where there is any religious sentiment amongst men at all, this sentiment incorporates itself with the law." Justice Story, in delivering the opinion of the court, said: "The Christian religion is truly a part of the common law of Pennsylvania." Similar declarations have been made by the courts of other states, among them by the New York Supreme Court (People v. Linden Miller, May 29, 1861), and by those of Delaware and New Jersey.

Speaking of the separation of church and state in our early American life, Dr. James H. Nichols, professor of church history in the University of Chicago, said in *The Christian Century* of March 3, 1948: "The community at large was Christian, indeed Puritan, and separation by no means signified any intent to weaken the hold of Christian ideology and morals on this community. The American Supreme Court consequently has spoken of this as a 'Christian nation.' [3] The Christian Sunday and holidays like Christmas and Thanksgiving are observed by public authority. Legislative assemblies have Christian chaplains, as do the armed services and public institutions. Marriage by Christian ministers is recognized by law when duly registered. Churches are subsidized by tax exemption. And most characteristic and important, the inner life and discipline of churches is recognized as beyond the jurisdiction of civil law." This is a pattern of separation which is benevolent rather than neutral to religion and contrasts strikingly with the situation found in lands where the church dominates the state.

[3] See U. S. Supreme Court decision in Trinity Church case, 143, U.S. 457.

Sectarianism vs. Christianity

The storm center of the church-state controversy has been the debated question of religious teachings and observances in our public schools and also the vexing problem of state aid, directly or indirectly, to schools which are not tax-supported. Many have contended that any sort of teaching about religion or even the reading of the Bible in our schools is in violation of the basic American principle of the separation of church and state. To refute that contention is one of the main purposes of this book.

The interpreters of our Constitution have clearly distinguished between the sectarianism which has divided us and the basic, underlying Christianity which unites us and which affords a basis of common understanding and fraternization between different religious groups. The Supreme Court of the United States has declared: "The term religion has reference to one's views of his relations to his Creator and to the obligations which they impose of reverence for His being and character and of obedience to His will. It is often confounded with the cultus or form of worship of a particular sect, *but is distinguishable from the latter.*" (Italics our own.)

The Standard Dictionary defines the word "sect" as "a body of persons distinguished by peculiarities of faith and practice from other bodies adhering to the same general system," and the word "sectarianism" is defined as "sectarian character or tendency; excessive devotion to or zeal for a particular sect." Our legislators and courts seemed until recently to have accepted the dictionary definitions of these terms as adequately expressing their intended meanings and distinctions. The difference between Christianity (the "general system") and sect is important because in nearly all of the state laws regarding religion in the public schools the prohibition is against the teaching of sectarian doctrines and not against the teaching of religion itself. It is this difference between sectarianism and basic Christianity which seems to offer a way out of the vexing educational dilemma into which our misguided zeal for religious liberty has led us and which, unfortunately, leaves 50% or more of our school-age population without any religious orientation whatever.

It is quite certain that the framers of the original anti-sectarian laws (which have furnished the model for practically all the other states which have passed similar legislation) did not intend to exclude religion itself from the schools, but only such teaching as might seem to favor a particular sect, or denomination, and thus promote religious dissension and infringe on human rights. This is evidenced by the fact that in Massachusetts, the first state to enact such legislation (the Massachusetts School Laws of 1826–1827), daily Bible reading in the public schools is still required by statute. This whole history is covered in Chapter III.

The ambiguity originates, not with the framers of the anti-sectarian laws, but with the interpreters thereof. Some state Supreme Courts (and in several instances attorneys general without court decision) have ruled against Bible reading in the schools and, in a few instances, even against the singing of religious hymns. Interpretations of identical or similar laws by different legal authorities are so conflicting that it is impossible to arrive at anything like a general consensus of opinion.

The Bible in the Public Schools

The whole controversy has seemed to center around the legality or illegality of reading the Bible in the public schools. Certain interests charge that the Bible is a sectarian book, a contention which has been sustained by a few courts, but denied by most. It is true that every sect looks to the Bible as the authority for its own particular tenets and as evidence against all opposing views, but it is also true that upon the general and fundamental teachings of the Bible practically all sects agree.

A 1949 report by the Research Division of the National Education Association on "The Status of Religious Education in the

Public Schools" states that a survey conducted by the U.S. Office of Education in 1929–1930 showed that eleven states and the District of Columbia required the reading of the Bible in the public schools. The eleven states were Massachusetts, Pennsylvania, Tennessee, New Jersey, Alabama, Georgia, Delaware, Maine, Kentucky, Florida, and Idaho, the last five of these states having passed compulsory legislation later than 1922.[4] The 1929–1930 survey showed that five states specifically permitted Bible reading and that in twenty other states it was generally considered lawful. In the twelve remaining states there was no legislation on the matter, but court decisions and the opinions of attorneys general or states' attorneys and of state superintendents regarded Bible reading as sectarian, and therefore as unlawful.

In practically all states where Bible reading is either enjoined or permitted, provision is made for the excusing of "conscientious objectors" from the room while such exercises are being conducted, a provision which would seem to obviate any possible objection to such a program but which also opens the way for all sorts of minority obstructionism. The courts of various states have been hampered by cases brought to suit by small minorities and even by individuals. Such cases, until the Champaign case, have with steady consistency been decided adversely to the complainants, but they have nevertheless served to clog the dockets of the courts and have cost the public fully as much as if there had been sound legal ground for the complaints.

It is the contention of this discussion that the possibility of such legal blocking and tackling by individuals or minority groups constitutes a real menace to democratic government, a basic principle of which is that majorities shall rule in the determination of public policies, a principle which should apply to educational policies as well as to matters political and economic. If it is possible for a small minority, or even for a single individual, to block

---

[4] Arkansas was added in 1930. (For further information, see Appendix, page 108.)

or defeat the will of the majority, then indeed it would seem that ours is a democracy only in name or in part.

If it is possible for an individual or a minority group to have the Bible excluded from the public schools on the ground that its use conflicts with their religious beliefs (or disbeliefs), there is no reason in principle why similar objections may not be interposed to exclude other textbooks and subjects as well. For instance, why should not certain groups be warranted in demanding elimination of all science textbooks which teach the theory of naturalistic evolution, claiming that such teachings violate their conscientious belief that God, by fiat, created the heavens and the earth and all things therein in six days of twenty-four hours each? Ghosts of the famous Scopes trial still haunt our memory.

If such objections may be raised against textbooks on religious grounds, why may they not also be raised on other grounds? Why may not social radicals complain against the teaching in our schools of economic and political theories which run counter to principles which to them are tantamount to a religion? The possibilities of such objections are endless if we once admit the right of minorities to obstruct or defeat the will of the majority in a community. Our school districts and school boards are practically autonomous and constitute the nearest approach to the democratic colonial "town meeting" that we have left in our American life. This basis of democracy should not lightly be allowed to become ineffective or obsolete. It appears increasingly likely that the last defensive stand of democracy will be made at the citadel of the public school board. If local majorities cannot secure their rights here, democracy will ultimately fail all along the line.

CHAPTER V

The Champaign Case and the First Amendment

It does not follow that one or more individuals have the right to have the courts deny the people the privilege of having their children instructed in the moral truths of the Bible because such objectors did not desire that their own children be participants therein. This would be to starve the moral nature of the many out of deference to the few.

——A decision of the courts of Texas (194 Texas)

There is nothing in the status of the public school, as an institution of the state, therefore, to render it godless. There is nothing in the principle of religious freedom or the separation of church and state to hinder the school's acknowledgment of the power and goodness of God. The common religious faith of the American people, as distinguished from the sectarian forms in which it is organized, may rightfully be assumed and find appropriate expression in the life and work of the public schools.

——**Luther A. Weigle,** Dean Emeritus of Yale Divinity School, in "Religion and Public Education," the report of a conference in Princeton, New Jersey, May 12-14, 1944.

THE QUESTION of church-state relationships has come to assume a gradual but ever-increasing significance in our national life, especially as sects increase and as the spirit of secularism continues to spread. For the most part, this question has been like the fires which ever smoulder in the heart of the globe, only occasionally manifesting themselves in seismic disturbances or in volcanic eruptions.

It is said that on thirteen different occasions Congress has faced this question in bills which have come before it, but all of these bills either died in committee or else otherwise failed of final passage. Not until November, 1947, has our federal Supreme Court attempted to face the full implications of the First Amendment to our Constitution with a view to interpreting its meaning as applied to a particular case brought before it. This was in connection with the famous "New Jersey Bus Case" [1] to the following general effect: "Neither a state nor the Federal Government can set up a church. Neither can pass laws which aid one religion, aid all religions, or prefer one religion over another. Neither can force or influence a person to go to or to remain away from church against his will or force him to profess a belief or disbelief in any religion. No person can be punished for entertaining or professing religious beliefs or disbeliefs, for church attendance or non-attendance. No tax, in any amount, large or small, can be levied to support any religious activities or institutions, whatever they may be called, or whatever form they may adopt to teach or practice religion. Neither a state nor the Federal Government can, openly or secretly, participate in the affairs of any religious organizations or groups and *vice-versa*. In the words of Jefferson, the clause against establishment of religion by law was intended

[1] Everson *v.* Board of Education, 330 U.S. 1.

to erect "a wall of separation between church and state." [2] This opinion, rendered in the Everson "bus case," assumed still greater importance, sixteen months later, as the judicial precedent for the Supreme Court decision in the Champaign case.

The first Amendment and its intended meaning will be more fully discussed in the last section of this chapter, but it may here be remarked that, in the opinion of many competent authorities, *only the Federal Congress* falls under the restrictions of the First Amendment, since matters of religion have not by the Constitution been committed to the Federal Government and therefore, under the Tenth Amendment, belong exclusively to the states. [3] Furthermore, it does not seem involved in the First Amendment that either the United States or the several states were ever intended to be debarred from giving aid to religion *in general*, so long as no disposition is shown to "prefer one religion over another." And we also join Justice Reed in the conviction that "a rule of law should not be drawn from a figure of speech" and that, therefore, the "wall of separation," referred to by Jefferson in a personal letter, can hardly be given the sweeping and authoritative significance attached to it by the Court.

To review briefly the incidents leading up to the federal Supreme Court decision in the Champaign case, the churches of Champaign, Illinois—Protestant, Catholic, and Jewish—with the endorsement and friendly coöperation of the public-school authorities, had since 1940 conducted weekday religious education classes on released time, in public-school buildings, and with the use of school facilities. Attendance on these classes was wholly voluntary.

Against this program a protest was entered by Mrs. Vashti McCollum, of Champaign, who petitioned through the courts that the public schools of that particular school district be ordered to discontinue the above described weekly half-hour Bible lessons

[2] Reynolds *v.* United States, *supra* at 164.
[3] See page 61.

conducted by the Champaign Council of Religious Education during school hours on released time, on written consent of the parents or guardians of the pupils. As the state courts decided, there was no invasion of the rights either of Mrs. McCollum or of her son, since her son had not attended the classes. However, Mrs. McCollum contended that her son was made to suffer embarrassment because his non-attendance made him the target of criticism by other pupils.

In a twenty-one page decision rendered by a three-judge court on January 26, 1946, the Court ruled that the Champaign classes in religion did not contravene the doctrine of the separation of church and state, that the weight of the evidence was against Mrs. McCollum's contention that her son had suffered embarrassment; and they also denied her claim that the course taught "tended to establish in the minds of pupils a belief in a certain God and Bible approved by the instructor."

The decision of the judges further read: "We have in the Supreme Court of the United States . . . an unmistakable authority for the proposition that the doctrine of the separation of church and state does not mean that there is any conflict between religion and the state in this country or any disfavor upon religion as such. It may therefore be said that, so far as federal constitutional provisions are concerned, and conceding that they are binding upon the State of Illinois and on the defendant school board, there is nothing in any expression of the federal Supreme Court that remotely indicates that there is any objection to the Champaign system of religious education."

The decision was thus a complete defeat for the petitioner on every count and a vindication of the honest effort which was being made by the churches of Champaign for the religious instruction of the largest possible number of the children and youth of the community, without public-school expense for textbooks, materials, or teachers.

Mrs. McCollum then appealed her case to the Illinois Supreme

Court which, on January 22, 1947, in Opinion No. 29678, upheld the decision of the lower court. This high state court found no indication of "any violation of state or federal guarantees." It also found that "such cases do not violate the freedom of conscience of any individual or group so long as classes are conducted on a purely voluntary basis." The decision further reads: "Our government very wisely refuses to recognize a specific religion, but this cannot mean that the government does not recognize or subscribe to religious ideals. We find such recognition in the very preamble of our State constitution. The government does not recognize a particular faith, but this cannot mean that it is indifferent to religious faith. To deny the existence of religious motivation is to deny the inspiration and authority of the Constitution itself." Up to this point in the story the courts, in dealing with the case, have defended the rights of the majority against sabotage by minorities and have upheld the rightful place of religion in our national culture. This decision of the State Supreme Court is all the more significant in view of the fact that the anti-sectarian laws of Illinois are about the most rigid anywhere to be found.

Mrs. McCollum then appealed her case from the State Court to the United States Supreme Court where it was admitted as No. 90, October term, 1947. Decision was rendered on March 8, 1948, by a vote of 8 to 1 in favor of the Appellant. However, the opinion of the court was by no means so unanimous as the vote might indicate. In addition to the out-and-out dissent of Justice Reed, there were also filed for record a supplemental opinion signed by four of the concurring Justices and an individual opinion filed by Justice Jackson which makes it difficult to understand how he could concur in the majority opinion.

Problems Arising from the Decision

In a number of respects the whole situation now seems even more confused and undefined than before the decision was rendered. While the majority did attempt to give an authoritative interpretation of the First and Fourteenth Amendments and to settle some questions which had been disturbing the public mind, it inferentially raised related questions which it did not clarify in any way whatever. For instance, some members of the court confessed inability to separate the secular from the religious in education, a differentiation which would seem fundamental to the whole matter at issue. In the second place, the decision left still undefined the legal status of the "released time" principle itself, an omission affecting approximately 2,700 weekday schools being conducted on released time away from public school properties, thus opening the way for endless litigation to clear up that point. That this decision has seriously embarrassed the whole "released time" enterprise is indicated by the result of a survey of such schools conducted by the National Educational Association, the results of which were made public in August, 1949. Questionnaires were sent to superintendents of 5,100 school systems which were answered by 2,639. Of those replying, 708, or about one-fourth, had a religious training program in operation, 1,621 had never had such a program, and 310 had stopped religious classes. Of the 310 communities to abandon religious training, 52.3% said the change came about because of the McCollum (Champaign) case.

Furthermore, the wide and comprehensive sweep of the majority opinion lends the suspicion that the Champaign case was merely the occasion for establishing a judicial precedent aimed at still more flagrant conditions in such situations as those in New Mexico, North Dakota, and North College Hill, Cincinnati, Ohio— a farflung reach of the decision which will probably be welcomed by a majority of citizens. It should be noted, however, that this particular decision applies only to the one specific school district in which the complaint originated, though the precedent thus established will doubtless be cited in similar cases arising in the future.

Discussion of the Champaign case has been all the more heated and general because, in the view of many, the court was probably both right and wrong. It was undoubtedly right in condemning a system which permitted the separation of pupils into sectarian groups and their instruction by sectarian teachers on school property and with the use of school facilities. Such practices are easily under suspicion of fostering sectarianism through the use of school property and personnel. But it is difficult for many people to see why the First Amendment should be expanded to prohibit also any friendly coöperation between the churches and the schools in the interest of community morals and morale and of the more general and complete cultural equipment offered through our public schools.

The most regrettable feature of the decision of the Supreme Court is the impetus which it will inevitably give to the already accelerating spread of secularism in our nation. To the rank and file of citizens the mandamus asked by Mrs. McCollum against any and every suggestion of religion in or through our public schools resolves itself into a duel between avowed atheism on the one hand and community religious education on the other, with atheism winning the decision, thus giving the green light to atheism and the red light to religion, an inference which no judicial disclaimer of such an intent can possibly dissipate.

That First Amendment

In all the discussions which have arisen concerning the Supreme Court's interpretation of the First Amendment to our national Constitution, we have seen nothing publicly reported which goes clear back to the meaning of that Amendment as it was interpreted by the framers thereof. To discover what they understood it to mean would seem fundamental to any later understanding of its purport, either by laymen or by judicial authorities for, after all, the Constitution means what its framers intended it to mean and not, as the late Chief Justice Hughes is reported to

have said, that "the Constitution means what the Supreme Court
says it means." Just what did the First Amendment mean to the
men who were influential in putting it into the Constitution?
Fortunately, we are not dependent on guesses or "prepossessions"
for our answer.

The Constitution of 1787 would probably never have been
ratified by the required number of states had it not been for the
assurance by Congress that a Bill of Rights would later be added
by way of amendment. Suggestions for such amendments began
to pour in from the states until the number finally reached a
total of 179. These suggested amendments passed for review into
the hands of James Madison, who had been giving special attention to the matter of amendments. On March 4, 1789, twelve
amendments, submitted by Madison, were adopted by a two-
thirds vote of both Senate and House and were sent to the states
for ratification. The first two of the proposed amendments failed
of ratification by the required number of states, but the remaining ten were accepted and thereby automatically became the first
ten Amendments to our Constitution—our "Bill of Rights."

The first of these Amendments (that containing the "establishment of religion" clause) has later been the subject of much discussion and debate as to its exact meaning and purport. This
Amendment was the undoubted work of James Madison and
Thomas Jefferson who, five years earlier, had jointly accomplished
in the Virginia Legislature the defeat of a bill intended to
establish the Episcopal Church as the legal religion of the state
and which proposed the levy of a general tax for its support.
Madison and Jefferson were thus well schooled in opposition to
a state-sponsored and state-controlled church.

In the course of Congressional discussion which changed the
First Amendment, as originally submitted, to its present form,
Madison said that he "apprehended the meaning of the words
to be that Congress should not establish a religion, and enforce
the legal observation of it by law, nor compel men to worship

God in any manner contrary to their conscience." [4] It is interesting to note that the word "national" was placed before the word "religion" in the original amendment but was finally omitted because of the fear that the emphasis upon a centralized national government might imperil the passage of the amendment. Madison's own interpretation of the meaning of the "establishment of religion" clause should make the meaning of the Amendment forever clear. This interpretation was urged by counsel for the defendants in the Champaign case, but the Supreme Court declined to accept their contention. Who was probably in the better position to interpret the meaning and intent of the First Amendment—Madison, who fathered the Amendment, or the Supreme Court, more than a century and a half later?

One thing in the First Amendment which prompts inquiry is the complete omission of any reference to the states. That very omission is significant in view of the Tenth Amendment, which was adopted at the same time and which reads: "The powers not delegated to the United States by the Constitution, nor prohibited by it to the states, are reserved to the states specifically, or to the people." Cooley's "Principles of Constitutional Law" says: "When a particular power is found to belong to the states, they are entitled to the same complete independence in its exercise as is the national government in wielding its own authority. Each within its own sphere has sovereign powers."

That it was the intention of the framers of the Constitution to keep religious issues forever out of federal jurisdiction and to leave them for state determination seems conclusive from statements of Thomas Jefferson. In his second inaugural address he said: "In matters of religion I have considered that its free exercise is placed by the Constitution independent of the Federal

---

[4] Annals of Congress, 8, pages 729–738; quoted by Watson on "The Constitution," Vol. 2, page 1373.

Government. I have therefore undertaken on no occasion to prescribe the religious exercises suited to it, but have left them as the Constitution found them, under the direction and discipline of the Church or State authorities acknowledged by the several societies." [5]

In 1808 Jefferson wrote to Rev. Dr. Miller: "I consider the government of the United States as interdicted by the Constitution from intermeddling with religious institutions, their doctrines, discipline, or exercises. This results not only from the provision that no law shall be made respecting the establishment or free exercise of religion, but from that also which preserves to the states the powers not delegated to the United States. Certainly no power to prescribe religious discipline has been delegated to the general government. It must then rest with the states, as far as it can in any human authority." [6]

From these unequivocal words of Thomas Jefferson there can be only one interpretation of the First Amendment as intended by the framers. If Jefferson was right, the appeal of Mrs. Vashti McCollum from the decision of the Supreme Court of Illinois might well have been dismissed by the federal Supreme Court on the ground of non-jurisdiction and as lacking any substantial federal question in the points at issue in the case.

NOTE—The most comprehensive and detailed analysis of the United States Supreme Court's decision in the Champaign case which has come to our notice is that presented by Dr. Charles Clayton Morrison in the three consecutive issues of *The Christian Century* for May 8, 15, and 22, 1949. A careful study of this analysis will richly repay anyone interested in this fundamental problem of American public education.

Another invaluable commentary on the United States Supreme Court decision in the Champaign case is the 169-page *Winter Quarterly*, 1949, published by the Duke University Law School under the title

[5] Watson on "The Constitution," Vol. 2, page 1381.
[6] From Samuel E. Forman's "Life and Writings of Thomas Jefferson," pages 360–361.

"Religion and the State." It is a symposium of eight chapters by eminent legal authorities and educators. The articles are mainly in criticism of the decision. The volume also contains chapters on "Religion and Federal Aid to Education" and on "Preferment of Religious Institutions in Tax and Labor Legislation."

CHAPTER VI

Religion as the Basis of a Broad Culture

We recognize today, more than yesterday, especially when the preservation of democracy has become a matter of life and death, the formative influence of the Judaic-Christian tradition in relation to what is richest and deepest in our inherited culture. . . . My plea is for as candid a study of the religious roots of our culture as we give to the secular—with no other purpose than to enable our youth to understand their own inheritance and to appreciate it as such. In no respect of the cultural heritage is the exclusion of religious studies more anomalous than in the failure to make our major religious classic, the English Bible, a part of the cultural equipment of every generation.

> ——F. Ernest Johnson, of Teachers'
> College, Columbia University, in
> an article on "Religion and
> Public Education" in *Information Service*, January 2, 1943.

Some day a book must be prepared by Catholics, Jews, and Protestants, presenting to American youth in the schools the spiritual heritage of our Western World—not as propaganda, but as basic knowledge—if they are to understand even where our democracy came from and what it means.

> ——Harry Emerson Fosdick to the
> Protestant Council of New York.
> (*Reader's Digest*, May, 1946)

Up to this point in our discussion the major emphasis on religion has been with respect to its indispensable relation to the improvement of the moral life of individuals and communities and upon bringing to the 50% or more of our school-age population, who are now untouched by any of the churches, some intelligent understanding of the part which religion has played in civilization and particularly in the development of our own national history.

Plutarch, Greek philosopher and biographer, wrote: "There never was a state of atheists. You may travel all over the world and you will find cities without walls, without king, without mint, without theater, without gymnasium; but you will nowhere find a city without God, without prayer, without oracles, without sacrifices. Sooner may a city stand without foundations than a state without belief in the gods. This is the bond of all society and the pillar of all legislation."

Every racial or national culture has been permeated by some sort of religion and it is impossible to understand the history of any people without knowing something of its religious background. This is particularly true of our own nation. Therefore, a study of the influence of religion upon our national development is an essential part of a complete cultural education. The challenge of religion to general education has been well stated by H. G. Wells in his "Outline of History" when he said: "Education is the preparation of the individual for society; and his religious training is the core of that preparation."

Wells' statement represents a point of view which in recent years has been finding increasing expression on the part of so-called secular educators, as well as on the part of religious leaders. In the trial-and-error course of our transition from church-sponsored to state-supported education, it has come about that religious interests have been left wholly to the churches and to allied agencies and that public education has considered itself entirely excused from any responsibility in the matter. That this segmental division of total education cannot permanently continue is the growing conviction, not only of religious leaders, but also of progressive workers in the field of general education.

In his book "The New Education and Religion," (1945) J. Paul Williams has this to say: "In view of the unquestioned intelligence and the unusual sensitivity of the leaders of the effort to achieve a new education, it is surprising that they ignore religion. Religion has no place in their philosophy, their plans, or their strategy. They design to introduce the child to the complete culture, but they leave out of their reckoning one of the most basic aspects of all the historic cultures; they wish to educate the whole child, but they refuse to consider one of his most fundamental needs; they aim to reach the basic motives of both men and societies, but they ignore the methods which, over and over again, have been shown to be the most effective in the control of actions and ideas." And in "Public Schools and Spiritual Values," [1] we read: "A program that consciously excludes religious development of the person is not concerned with the development of the whole person any more than a program that consciously excludes esthetic development would be."

In an address delivered by F. Ernest Johnson, of Teachers' College, Columbia University, at the joint meeting of interchurch organizations in Cleveland, Ohio, on December 9, 1942, he said: "To exclude religion from the study of contemporary life is a sort of negative indoctrination, or indoctrination by default, a silent testimony that the community considers religion the one phase of its common life which is not worth bringing within the range of intelligent interest. . . . Failure to condition a young life by rooting it in rich soil is a crime against youth." And Lecomte

[1] Brubacher *et al*, 1945.

du Noüy says in his "Human Destiny": "To give children an intellectual tincture, a smattering of 'instruction' without previously constructing on firm moral foundations the base which must support it, is to build on sand; and the higher the monument the more complete will be its collapse."

In the *American School Board Journal* for December, 1946, appears a significant statement by Herbert B. Mulford, a widely known authority on public-school board administration. He says: "This problem [religion in the schools] has a long and difficult history. Parochial and private schools have solved it only in part. Attention is being called to leadership for this field through the demand of the clergy to do something more than secular in training for moral values and in the marked activities under the so-called Gary Plan of teaching religion on school premises or elsewhere permissively on released or dismissed time. The nubbin of the whole argument seems to be that *if educators wished it accomplished,* there would be no legal barrier to solution of the problem. Broadly speaking, it seems to be assumed that state constitutions are against religion in the schools. *This seems to be contrary to facts.* The basic problem seems to be to know the difference between ethics through secular teaching and morality based on religious faith. At present leadership in this field (the public school) simply defaults." (Italics our own)

The December, 1946, issue of the *Phi Delta Kappan,* devoted entirely in this issue to "Education, Religion, and Democracy," contains a score of articles by leading educators. Of these writers, one-third either directly or inferentially declare that religion is the basis of democracy and must be included in education. Says J. Wesley Bratton, "Democracy and Christianity are so closely bound together that democracy has been called the political expression of Christianity on earth. It follows that the inclusion of Christian concepts in the school curriculum is the responsibility of education if democracy is to survive."

The proper aim of education is not primarily to impart information, but to develop the pupil's character and his appreciation of all the finest things in life—literature, history, science, music, art, and beauty in all of its forms, including "the beauty of holiness." The public schools are doing a splendid work in developing the aesthetic appreciations, but they are doing nothing at all, formally and officially, to develop appreciation of life's very deepest interest, religion. To try to develop the other appreciations and at the same time to leave religion out of the total cultural picture is like trying to develop one side of an athlete's body while leaving the other side in a state of total atrophy. Until this situation is remedied, public education cannot claim to offer a complete culture to its students nor can we expect to develop respect for law and order while giving no official heed to the foundations of moral character.

In the *International Journal of Religious Education* for November 1940, page 13, Dr. George A. Coe says: "Why should the public schools be at all reticent with respect to the religious factor in our culture? Why not include in the study of history an outline of the development of religion as well? Why not make pupils acquainted with the churches in the community, as well as with the fire department? Why not open to pupils the contrasts among sects, just as the best schools now handle various problems? Why should not intelligent appreciation of religion be cultivated, as well as an intelligent appreciation of our country? Appreciation, that is, through analytical understanding of contrasts and alternatives? That is the democratic way of dealing with any social question; it is the way that religion will be handled by the public schools whenever they become unqualifiedly democratic. The principle of separation of churches from the taxing power would not be violated thereby, for this principle does not exclude religion, but only sectarianism, and a fully democratic handling of religion would be the exact opposite of a sectarian handling of it."

The foregoing citations, all of them appearing since 1939, are indicative of a new trend of thinking in the educational discussions of the present day. A quarter of a century ago such expressions could hardly have gotten a hearing even in church circles, but today leaders in public education as well as in religious education are becoming increasingly aware of the very real problem involved in the segmental and disunited character of the total program of education. With no unity of plan and with no unified administration, it can hardly be expected that disconnected and unrelated efforts can produce the well-defined results at which total education should aim. The record of crime and juvenile delinquency alone is of itself sufficient to raise serious doubts as to the effectiveness of our present bifurcated educational system, a doubt which has been gathering force as we have come to realize the growing spread of secularism in our American life during the last three-quarters of a century.

We are now beginning to make several frank recognitions: (1) of the necessity of making basic moral and religious education universal; (2) of the importance of making it an integral part of the unitary educational experience of the pupil instead of treating it as something separated from his daily life and as optional and of questionable value; (3) of the inadequacy of the church program of religious education from the standpoint both of trained teaching personnel and also of the time devoted to this basic interest; (4) of the illogical separation of basic religious orientation from the education provided by the state; and (5) of the fact that to put basic moral and religious guidance into the very foundation of public-school education is the only way by which we can hope to develop religious appreciations in the 50% or more of our school-age population now untouched by any church agency.

The Problem of Curriculum

One of the major difficulties to be encountered in connection with such a proposal will be the initial lack of a curriculum which, while covering the basic elements of religion, will yet be sufficiently non-sectarian to win the approval at least of Protestants, Catholics, and Jews and which will be so planned as to command a more representative share of the pupil's time than is now provided by any agency outside of the parochial schools. This is a task which will challenge the most capable leadership both in the churches and also in the public schools, but it definitely can be done when once its necessity is recognized. At present religion is out of the schools largely because so many people assume that it cannot be taught without sectarian bias. Once demonstrate that an acceptable curriculum is possible, and such objections will become practically negligible. In "Public Schools and Spiritual Values," [2] we read: "Whenever and wherever the leaders of the various churches agree that the creeds and the rival claims and practices of religion can be studied by the ordinary empirical processes of the other work of the public schools, little difficulty will be experienced in making a study of these aspects of religion also a part of the program of public education." In addressing the Missouri State Teachers' Association in 1941, Dr. Charles Clayton Morrison said: "When it is once demonstrated that religion can be taught in a manner acceptable to Catholic, Protestant, and Jew—yes, and to that portion of the community which is not attached to any sect—the problem will be potentially solved."

In a previously quoted statement of Mr. Herbert B. Mulford to the effect that "the basic problem seems to be to know the difference between ethics through secular teaching and morality based on religious faith," it may be that we have pointed out for us the key to our approach to the curriculum problem. There seems to be no objection from any quarter to the teaching of morality in our public schools, though there seems to be considerable confusion as to the manner and matter of instruction.

Much emphasis is being laid by a recent group of educational

[2] Brubacher *et al*, page 72.

philosophers on the "spiritual values" implicit in our public-school curriculums, but little of general effort has been made to point out those values or to show teachers how to utilize them. The most outstanding and fruitful effort along this line which has come to our notice is the project carried out by the public schools of Los Angeles in 1944–1945. Complaints were made by parents to the school board that their children were learning little of manners and less of morals in the schools. As a result Mrs. Emma Pixley, a teacher of English, was asked by the school superintendent to see what could be done about the matter. She undertook to appraise the school curriculum in terms of its "spiritual values" and then published a 112-page booklet explaining her idea, that the intangibles should be taught along with the tangibles, and pointing out the possibilities in the various courses of study. So fruitful were the results of this program that the Los Angeles school board made Mrs. Pixley's position permanent and conferred on her the title of "Supervisor of Moral and Spiritual Values for the Public Schools of Los Angeles." Such a program as that of Los Angeles could and should be carried out in every community or school district, and guidance should be afforded to teachers in utilizing opportunities within the curriculum for emphasizing moral and spiritual values.

The junior high school of Highland Park, Texas, has approached the problem from a still different angle. Instead of seeking out and utilizing the "spiritual values" to be found in the curriculum, a wholly extra-curricular approach has been made. Following the installation of a new public address system throughout the school, Miss Maude McElvaney, music teacher in the school, conceived the idea of utilizing the opening of the school day, in each home-room, for five or six minutes of meditation. The programs are carefully prepared and are approved by the principal before being presented. They are designed, not for indoctrination, but to fit actual life problems. Broadcast from the studio and control room just off the principal's office, the program opens promptly at nine o'clock with a hymn recording, calling more than one thousand pupils to reverent attention. Thanks to a Texas law which permits the reading of the Bible without comment, the hymn is followed by a verse of Scripture and this, in turn, by a brief meditation which is *not* an exposition of the verse just read. Hymn, verse, and meditation are all made to point in the same direction and then are climaxed by a brief prayer of thanksgiving and resolution. The whole program occupies no more than five or six minutes, but experience has proven that it gives a fine atmosphere in which to begin the day's study and that it is a direct contribution to pupil morale. In this way the whole school receives thirty minutes a week of spiritual stimulation which is doubtless of greater value than the thirty-five to fifty-nine minutes possible under the released-time plan—*and it is given daily.* This program completely solves the problem of capable teaching service and there is not the faintest odor of sectarianism. The plan has not only met with no objection but with wholesale approval, and requests for information have come from eighteen states and from Hawaii. For an extended presentation of the plan, see the article "One School Unafraid of Religion" in the January, 1950, *Christian Herald.*

The grave danger in all education is that the vital character ends which should be kept in view by all teachers and administrators will fail of observation simply because they have nowhere been clearly indicated in the curriculum, nor has any effective aid been given to teachers leading them to the discovery of opportunities for moral training. Several years ago I asked the president of a municipal school board in a leading university center of the midwest what there was in the curriculum of his schools in the way even of instruction in morals. After a moment of reflection he replied, "Nothing at all." His reply occasioned no surprise for, in the "enrichment" of the curriculum along scientific and aesthetic lines, it has been easy to overlook the moral and spiritual aims which must underlie all true culture.

If there is any one basic aim which should motivate our entire educational system, it is the inculcation in our future citizens of sound moral principles and ethical ideals. Such instruction may indeed fall short of strictly religious content, but its value can never be lost, for there is a direct and inevitable connection between moral training and religious beliefs and practices. If one starts from the basis of moral principles, he will eventually find himself facing the challenge and implications of religion; if he starts on the basis of religious instruction, he will find himself all along the way facing the precepts and principles of morality. Indeed, one is led to question whether morals have evolved from religion or religion from morals. Certain it is that conscience and moral convictions must have taken form considerably in advance of religious or philosophical formulations. Democritus (c. 499– c. 357 B.C.), Socrates (c. 467–c. 399 B.C.), Plato (c. 427–c. 347 B.C.), and Aristotle (c. 384–c. 322 B.C.) are usually regarded by students of ethics as being the founders of their science. But eight centuries before the time of these philosophers the Ten Commandments embodied a system of morality which must have won the approval of the best elements of mankind ages before the Ten Commandments were written into a code and fortified by the sanctions of religion.

There is no recorded period of history in which murder, theft, perjury, and adultery have not been looked upon with public disapproval or even punished by law, neither has there been any historic age in which reverence for parents has not been extolled. Thus it would seem that thorough instruction in morals is a solid foundation on which a superstructure of religious orientation may be based. The introduction of such studies into the public school curriculum would doubtless serve to abate many of the evils which are conspicuous in our present American life, and at the same time, without any suspicion whatever of sectarianism, would help to create an attitude of open-mindedness toward religion.

In an article in *The Rotarian Magazine* by Mr. J. Edgar Hoover, he makes this significant statement: "There are many contributory causes of juvenile delinquency such as the breakdown of the home as an institution, the general spirit of our war-time abandon, the sharply increased spending power of inexperienced youth, and the 'war hero' spirit of those not old enough to serve. *However, the real underlying problem which allows these forces to produce juvenile delinquents is one of defective mental attitudes.* (Italics our own.) . . . The mental attitudes which are usually absent among boys and girls involved in juvenile crime are old-fashioned but fundamental principles which are as old as the history of civilized man:

1. *Honesty*—telling the truth—being on the square with associates, parents and teachers;

2. *Respect for parents*—and, of course, there is the reciprocal responsibility of the parents conducting themselves so as to warrant respect;

3. *Fair play*—on the sand lot, at home, and in the school room;

4. *Sense of decency*—in thinking, speech, and conduct. This is a mental attitude which also requires development among many adults before they can be called exemplary instructors of youth;

5. *Respect for law and order*—on the street, in the school, and at home;

6. *Religious activity*—gaining a fundamental knowledge of the religions which make a life of service the most satisfying life of all;

7. *Willingness to work*—for what one receives;

8. *Willingness to finish the job*—to follow through regardless of the difficulties and hardships encountered;

9. *As much schooling as possible*—Dissatisfaction toward school and truancy from classes are well-known factors contributing to careers of juvenile delinquency;

10. *Ambition*—to achieve distinction in a chosen career."

In pointing to attitudes as the basis of character, Mr. Hoover is putting himself directly in line with the best psychology of the modern day and, in the above enumeration of attitudes which should be inculcated in our children and young people, he is also putting himself squarely on the foundation of religious principles; for where would we go for a steady and consistent emphasis on such attitudes except to religion? It is such attitudes as the above which, with consistent uniformity, result from Christian training and which are of such fundamental importance that it would seem no possible objection could be lodged against them. Such attitudes should be definitely inculcated in *all* American boys and girls, and the public school seems to be the only place where such training can be made universal.

The objection has been raised that Christianity is only one among many competing cults and that it would be impossible to frame a curriculum which would be acceptable to all. In answer to this objection it may be said that the Sunday School lessons, in almost universal use throughout the United States and Canada, have been coöperatively outlined by over forty Protestant denominations composing the International Council of Religious Education. Since these denominations represent a large part of the Protestant church membership of North America, their coöperation in curriculum-making represents a high degree of religious unanimity.

But any religious curriculum for the public schools would have to be even more free from controversial or sectarian matters than are these lessons of the International Council, for account must be taken also of at least two other religious groups besides Protestantism—the Roman Catholics and the Jews. But after all controversial matters between these groups are counted out, there is still remaining an underlying groundwork of religious faith concerning which there has never been any debate outside of pure atheism. As Dr. Luther A. Weigle has pointed out,[3] "Underlying all our differences, America has a common religious faith—common not in the sense that everybody shares it, for there are some among us who deny or ignore God; but in the sense that it is common to the three great religious groups—Protestant, Catholic, and Jewish—to which the great majority of American citizens belong. These citizens—Protestant, Catholic, and Jew—worship the one

[3] "Religion and Public Education."

God, Creator of all things and Father of all men. They believe that His will has been revealed in the life and literature of the Hebrew people as this is recorded in the Bible and that it is discernible in nature about us and in conscience within. They acknowledge the principle of human duty as set forth in the Ten Commandments, in the teaching of the Hebrew prophets, in the Golden Rule, and in the law of love to God and to fellow-men. They can all unite in the Lord's Prayer: 'Our Father who art in heaven . . . Thy Kingdom come, Thy will be done.' "

As the matter now stands, schools generally hold themselves entirely aloof from the whole subject of religion, a situation which results in making the school unwittingly an agent of secularism, that is, of atheism. It thus comes about that pupils do not receive from the public schools any impulse or suggestion which would lead them to seek religious nurture from any source whatever. There should be a definite acknowledgement on the part of the public schools of a responsibility to bring to their pupils a *complete and inclusive* culture, embracing such information as will enable them to make intelligent religious choices and to develop an appreciation of the part which religion has played in the life and history of mankind. It is perfectly possible for the schools to supply a groundwork of factual knowledge of religion around which the denominations could each build its own body of sectarian instruction.

To advance beyond purely moral and ethical teachings, such as are suggested by Mr. J. Edgar Hoover,[4] without any sectarian bias whatever, the public schools could inculcate an appreciation of religion as an essential part of general culture, including a consideration of such things as the following:

1. Of an overruling power, higher than ourselves, whom we know as God, who has created the heavens, the earth, and all things therein;

2. Of God as the source of the moral order, whose will should be our law, and to whom we are morally responsible;

[4] See pages 73-74.

3. Of God as the author and giver of every good and perfect gift and as the beneficent and providential guardian of our lives;

4. Of God as the Father of *all* men, in whose sight men are of more importance than sparrows, sheep, Sabbaths, or holy days;

5. Of ourselves and of all men as God's children and therefore as all brothers and sisters, regardless of race, nationality, language, color, or creed and as having equal rights with ourselves in God's sight;

6. Of the Golden Rule as the only fair and secure basis of human relationships and, therefore, of democracy;

7. Of our consequent obligations to those who are less fortunate than ourselves, and to other races and nationalities in our own land and beyond the seas;

8. Of a life of unselfish service to mankind as the highest end of self-realization and as the only effective way of serving God;

9. Of all those virtues of character which make for helpful, coöperative living, and for good citizenship;

10. And, finally (or possibly firstly), of the Bible as a record of man's experience of God through the ages and as "a lamp unto our feet and a light unto our path."

Since these fundamentals of religious truth are accepted by an overwhelming majority of American citizens in all of the churches and even outside of the churches, simple democratic principles and sound statesmanship would suggest that these basic religious teachings should become a part of the cultural education of all our American boys and girls whenever individual communities so elect.

And so we might go on amplifying and enriching our non-sectarian curriculum of religious education. The field is limitless, the opportunity is propitious, the need is great. We believe that conference and experimentation would develop a curriculum of fundamental religious principles which could be taught on a strictly non-sectarian basis and without touching on a single item of controversial debate. This whole matter of a properly graded curriculum would afford a fine field of study for graduate seminar groups in theological schools, schools of religious education, normal schools, teachers' colleges, etc.

If the basic principles and truths of religion are not definitely taught, and taught to *all* of America's children and young people, they will not be accidentally acquired in the rough and tumble struggle of our modern competitive system nor in the present secularized condition of our national life. It is difficult to see how anyone except pure atheists could object to the teaching of such things in our public schools, especially since there does not appear any other way in which such training can ever be brought to the 50% or more of our school-age population who are not under the tutelage of any of the churches and who are extremely unlikely to receive such teaching from any source other than our public schools.

CHAPTER VII

The American Council on Education Speaks

With publication of the Report of the Committee on Religion and Education, one is tempted to say a new day has dawned in educational thinking and writing. Here at last is a treatise constructive, purposeful, and direct. Only the richest superlatives of the language are fit to describe the forthright thinking and clear expression of this report. It is a significant document, perhaps the most significant yet published by the American Council on Education. Certainly nothing written in this generation by diplomats, sociologists, or scientists, is more important for the cure of the ills that beset our times.

A Catholic educator is also an American citizen and considers himself a part of American education. Because he loves his country as a citizen should, he is deeply concerned that all American youth possess a knowledge and understanding of the rich religious sources from which the American way of life has developed. He can only rejoice if a way is found to include the study of religion and religious institutions in public education.

——Excerpt from a statement by
Rev. Thomas J. Quigley, Superintendent of the Catholic School
Board of the Diocese of Pittsburgh, Pennsylvania. (Published
in the May-June, 1947, issue of
Religious Education)

IN APRIL, 1947, there was published the report of a special Committee of the American Council on Education, appointed to formulate a statement on "The Relation of Religion to Public Education, The Basic Principles." In the foreword of that report, Mr. George F. Zook, President of The American Council, makes the following explanatory statement:

In the spring of 1944, the American Council on Education, with the coöperation of the National Conference of Christians and Jews, assembled a group of educators at Princeton, N. J., to discuss the relation of religion to public education. The conference included unofficial representatives of education on the elementary, secondary, and higher levels, under both public and private auspices, and leaders of the three major faiths in the United States. The purpose of the meeting was to exchange views on a matter of increasing concern to educators as well as to religious leaders and a considerable part of the lay public.

Following this meeting, which confined itself to its task and recommended no specific policy or program, the American Council on Education created the Committee on Religion and Education to conduct or instigate such studies and educational activities in this area as might stimulate informed thinking. The Committee undertook as its first task the preparation of the document here presented. The first purpose of the Committee was to identify and define the issues that arise in considering the issues that arise between religion and public education in America in the light both of our educational history and of the total cultural pattern. It then undertook to analyze the existing situation and to state some broad principles which it is hoped will find a large measure of acceptance and which will stimulate constructive criticism and experimentation.

The report of this Committee was made public in April, 1947, as Volume II, of the American Council's Series I—Reports of Committees and Conferences, No. 26. It was also reprinted in the May–June, 1947, issue of *Religious Education*, which devotes the entire issue to this report and to reviews of the same by fifteen prominent educators and religious leaders, representing both favorable and unfavorable comment.

The report itself constitutes a document which, in the educational field, is comparable only to the Magna Carta and the Declaration of Independence in the development of democracy. It calls attention to the general secularization of life in the Western World and to the concurrent secularization of education and its consequences, pointing out that the present exclusion of religion from our public schools was the thing farthest from the intention of those who were active in the endeavor to banish sectarianism from the schools.

The report offers a definition of religion in these words: "In simple terms religion implies an ultimate reality to which supreme allegiance must be given," and it also further states "we believe the responsibility of public education with reference to religion is determined by fidelity to the culture in its entirety."

The Committee also attempts to define what it means by "teaching," summing up its philosophy in these words: "To be educated does not mean to have been taught what to think, but it does mean to have learned what to think *about* and to have acquired definite convictions with respect to values," and it further states, "Our purpose at this point is to urge consideration by educators of the possibility of raising the ban on religious subject matter to the extent that the study of it can be guided, as is the case in those schools which most successfully direct the study of other materials about which divergent views are recognized."

The report does not view with favor the proposal to teach "a common core of religious belief," since that phrase suggests a "watering down" of the several faiths involved, a result which would be universally deprecated. But, the report states, "We who make this report believe that the American people are deeply, though not always articulately, conscious of a religious heritage to whose central values they want their children to be committed. . . . The criterion of acceptance in the curriculum is not universal agreement; rather it may be said that the presumption is in favor of inclusion in the school curriculum of any area of interest that lends itself to objective study if a *substantial portion of the constituency of the schools regard it as of vital concern."* (Italics our own)

The Committee puts itself on record as recognizing the validity of current defenses which are being made of our public schools on the ground that they foster "spiritual values," but it also maintains that "spiritual values" do not embody the full, valid content of religion. "No person is fully educated who has not gained a knowledge of the faiths men live by. And unless the schools are content to leave one of the major areas of life unexplored, the specifically religious beliefs and aspirations of human beings must have attention."

The report argues that entirely to exclude the study of religion from the public schools is in itself a form of sectarianism. "To vast numbers of Americans the denial of the supernatural in the classroom is a negation of their faith and to make such a denial is to bring religion into the schools with a vengeance. . . . Religious people have every right to resent and resist an attack on their faith made in the name of academic scholarship. . . . Negative religious dogmatism in the schools is as un-American as positive religious dogmatism."

The report calls attention to the wide diversity of practice in relation to the schools, a situation which reveals that there is no fixed or consistent policy. There are almost as many states which require the reading of the Bible in the schools as there are those which prohibit it. "In some states more explicit forms of worship are prescribed and in innumerable instances simple services of worship are conducted with evident community approval. Many states allow school credit for Bible studies conducted outside the school. Some school systems permit religious classes in the school, maintained by private contributions. Weekday religious education conducted by the churches, with only a minimum of school cooperation, is widely popular." The report says, "The situation may be interpreted as indicating that there is in fact an 'American way' in education with respect to religion, namely, state and local control, with freedom to experiment. This is as it should be. *Public education in this country is a function of the states, whose policy it is to delegate control in large part to the local community.*" (Italics our own.)

On the matter of the separation of church and state the report goes on record as saying that "there is no such thing as a completely free church in a free state." The church is subject to the state in a variety of ways and the church, in turn, is recognized and its services are utilized by the state in governmental affairs, such as the employment of chaplains, the maintenance of religious services in public hospitals, prisons, etc. The Committee concludes this section of its report by saying: "The core of meaning in the doctrine of separation of church and state we believe to be this: there shall be no ecclesiastical control of political functions; there shall be no political dictation in the ecclesiastical sphere except as public safety or public morals may require it. *This doctrine may not be invoked to prevent public education from determining on its merits the question how religious phases of the culture shall be recognized in the school program.*" (Italics our own)

The popularity of weekday church schools is cited as an evidence of community interest in religious education, but it is recognized that this plan is inadequate to solve the fundamental problems involved. "It is not to be confused with the function of the public school. Its indefinite extension would not of itself modify the conception we are here defending of the scope and adequacy of the public school program. At most it would be complementary." Moreover, "the released-time program is not directly related to the problem with which this report is concerned. *We are addressing ourselves to the responsibility of the schools in their own right, and in relation to their own program.*" (Italics our own)

The basic responsibility of the schools is "to give the young an understanding of the culture and an appreciation of the ideals, values, and institutions which the culture cherishes. . . . We hold no program of general education to be adequate that leaves any large area of human interest untouched." There is pointed out the difference between acquiring factual information, on the one hand, and the gaining of a meaningful learning experience on the other. All wholesome education is "induction into the life of one's world through continuous, meaningful, and rewarding participation. . . . If society is really concerned, as we believe it increasingly is today, that religion should have a more important place in the lives of its youth, a first step is to break through the wall of ignorance about religion and to increase the number of contacts with it. . . . It is a grave mistake to suppose that the public school . . . can be neutral in the matter. . . . It is not the business of public education to secure adherence to any particular religious system or philosophical outlook. But we believe that it is the business of public education to impel the young toward a vigorous, decisive personal reaction to the challenge of religion."

As to what can be done in the way of religious study within the public schools, the report says: "in certain communities almost anything seems to be possible. . . . Advances in public policy have to come about where the community is ready for it." It is pointed out that religion may well have a place among the social studies, along with government, markets, labor, industry, welfare, etc. Likewise, the Bible as literature may well have a place in English studies, even allowing pupils to use whatever version they may prefer. "In history, in the sciences, and in philosophy, religion comes into the picture. . . . It is of the essence of our position that religion is inseparably bound up with the culture as a whole. . . . We believe that a total orientation toward religion as a part of the culture is better accomplished if religion is not abstracted from those fields of study, however designated in the curriculum of which it is a part."

The report goes on to deal with the importance of teacher education, with religion and education at the college level, with the school, the church, and the home, as related to each other, and with the spiritual replenishment of modern culture. But the foregoing rather sketchy abstract and interpretation is sufficient for our purpose here; the citations chosen for presentation are those which illuminate the foregoing chapters of this book. The important thing to note in this report, next to the content itself, is that here we find the most influential and authoritative educational body in the country putting itself on record in this forthright and unequivocal way on the most outstanding and most discussed educational problem of the present day. The document will certainly blaze new trails for educational policy in the future. The abstract here made is given for two purposes: (1) to confirm the positions taken in the foregoing chapters and (2) to disseminate as widely as possible the convictions set forth in the report.

The entire report, as printed in full in the May-June, 1947, issue of *Religious Education*, should be read by everyone at all interested in the general subject. Especially valuable are the evaluations of the report by fifteen well-known educators and religious leaders, both pro and con. Possibly the one which will be the most challenging, as indicating support from a generally unanticipated quarter, is that of the Rev. Thomas J. Quigley, superintendent of the Catholic School Board of the Diocese of Pittsburgh, Pennsylvania, quotation from whose statement was made at the beginning of this chapter.

CHAPTER VIII *The Challenge to the Schools*

If 50% of the public school population is not now under the influence of the church schools of religion, then it might be expected that the public schools which they do attend should supply this deficiency and do it in a way that is legal.

——Conrad A. Hauser, in "Teaching Religion in the Public School" (p. 160)

The very life of our civilization is at stake. The American school as it first reared its log walls in the wilderness villages of New England was religious through and through. The favor with which the non-religious state school is regarded is, I verily believe, due to the thoughtlessness of the moment and will not last. I would permeate the regular state school with the religion of the majority, be that religion as Protestant as Protestantism itself.

——Archbishop Ireland to the N.E.A. at Minneapolis, Minn., 1890. (*Proceedings of the N.E.A.*, St. Paul, Minn., 1890, pages 179-184)

IN CHAPTER II there was outlined the course of events whereby the early church-sponsored schools of our nation gradually gave place to tax-supported public schools under the sponsorship and supervision of the several states. That this change of responsibility has resulted materially (1) in the wider diffusion of education and (2) in the more general and complete development of its principles and methods, no one would be bold enough to deny. But it is a distinct loss to education that, in the transition from church-sponsored to state-sponsored education, emphasis shifted from basic moral aims to the newly developing findings and methods of material science. This shift of emphasis need not have been. In taking over control of popular education, the states should have assumed the *entire* cultural responsibility and not have permitted basic character aims to become eclipsed.

No education can be regarded as complete or effective which fails to give primary place to character aims and to definite inculcation of moral principles. In no other way can we hope to rear generations of right-minded and useful citizens. The very life of democracy and the security of our nation are dependent upon the moral character of successive generations of our American boys and girls. Americans may rightfully look to their public schools to offer to their pupils a type of education which, to a convincing degree, will turn out young men and women so well-grounded in moral principles and civic ideals that there will no longer be possible the riotous carnival of juvenile delinquency and crime which the statistics of our federal Department of Justice reflect. The present crime situation is in itself an emergent reason for the introduction into our public school system of *every* element of instruction and training which might lead to a reversal of the criminal and secular trends in our national life. And there are few who would dare venture to deny the beneficial contribution which thorough moral and religious instruction in our public schools would make to our national life and character.

While the set-up in the several states varies somewhat, the general policy is for the state Office of Education to leave everything to local determination so long as minimum state standards are met. Thus it comes to pass that education develops from the bottom upward, rather than from the state office downward. It is therefore literally true that the local public school board of district or municipality, as the case may be, is the purest example of democracy still to be found in our American commonwealth. It may easily become the citadel at which the last defensive stand of democracy will be made.

The base upon which our whole educational structure rests is the local public-school board. It is intrenched in a position of autonomy, not only by continuous custom from the beginning of our system of free public schools, but also by an amplitude of judicial decisions. This is illustrated by the following citations from the Illinois Supreme Court decision in the Champaign case: "School boards have a wide discretion in the exercise of powers conferred upon them, and the courts will not interfere with the judgment of the board unless by an arbitrary and discretionary action the powers granted are abused. . . . Questions of policy are solely for the determination of the board, and when they have once been determined by it the courts will not inquire into their propriety." [1] Also the following: "Courts will not interfere with the judgment of the board unless by an arbitrary and discriminatory action it abuses the power granted." [2] This situation is as it should be, and is the only way in which the local program of education can be made to fit local conditions and needs.

The local public-school board, whether of district or municipality, thus becomes the final authority in the administration of school policies, curriculum, and personnel, except when the plan-

[1] People ex rel. Fursman v. City of Chicago, 278 Ill. 318, 116, N.E. 158.
[2] Segar v. Board of Education, 317 Ill. 418, 148, N.E. 289.

ning and determination of curriculum may, by the action of the board, be delegated to the faculty, as is done by many modern schools throughout the country. This wide authority, given to and through the public school board, opens up the widest possible opportunity for experiment in education and for the consequent improvement of the curriculum and its adaptation to the wishes and needs of the local constituency. What the constituency wants it can have, if and when approved by the school board.

It is agreed by many students of the United States Supreme Court decision in the Champaign case that, while the decision definitely estops *the churches* from entering the public schools for the purpose of teaching religion, there is not a single word in the decision which prevents *the schools themselves* from doing so on their own responsibility in fulfillment of their obligation to present to their pupils a *complete* education and an adequate preparation for intelligent and effective citizenship. There is thus a direct challenge to the schools to fulfill the educational functions which the churches are estopped from performing. The decision is to be welcomed in that the public schools, now as never before, are compelled to face the full implications of their educational responsibilities. It is fervently to be hoped that the new situation will stimulate the schools to a fresh appraisal of their total task and that there will result a wide experimentation on their part in all sorts of local situations in the hope that a sane and satisfactory way may be found for filling in this illogical gap in our American public educational system.

Two statements have been published within the last year (1949) both of which have an important bearing on what may be done and what may not be done in the way of teaching religion in the public schools. Both of these statements give support to criticisms of the Supreme Court decision in the Champaign case as being unwarrantably sweeping in its scope.

The first of these documents, "The Status of Religious Education in the Public Schools," issued by the National Education

Association in June, 1949, draws an important distinction which seems to make it possible for the public schools to make an *objective* study of religion an integrated part of the regular curriculum. The report makes a clear distinction between instruction *about* religion as contrasted with the teaching of sectarian doctrines. It says: "In connection with the public schools, there are two common meanings to the expression 'religious education.' It may mean the imparting of knowledge about religions or it may mean the inculcation of beliefs, practices, and attitudes of particular religions." This is a difference in meanings of which the Supreme Court took absolutely no notice and which apparently leaves the objective teaching *about* religion perfectly constitutional and legal.

The other document is the October 25, 1949, issue of the *School Board News Bulletin* of the Illinois Association of School Boards, which devotes more than one-sixth of its total space to a clarification of the present status of religious education in the public schools in the light of the Supreme Court's decision in the Champaign case. The statement concludes: "The following conclusions seem to be warranted: (1) A board of education may not permit religious education classes to be taught in the school buildings during the time when school is in session or when the building is being used for school purposes. (2) A school board may not release pupils from their educational pursuits on condition that they attend classes in religious education in lieu of attendance of the public schools. (3) A school board may not help to promote pupils for religious classes in any manner whatsoever or take any active part through its teachers or superintendents in the supervision of or provision for classes in religious education. (4) *The decision does not prohibit the teaching of factual information of the history and tenance of religious bodies in the regular curriculum.* (5) The Constitutionality of section 6-43 of the School Code giving school boards the power to grant the temporary use of school buildings when not occupied by schools for religious meetings and Sunday Schools were not passed upon by the Court. Probably such use by the school buildings is not illegal provided the school furnishes no funds and is required to pay no expense in connection with such use." (Italics supplied) The foregoing citations show clearly how wide a discretionary power is still invested in school boards *under the law*. The decision bans some widespread practices which are clearly questionable, but it does *not* banish either religion or the objective teaching *about* religion by the schools themselves in the regular curriculum. The road is still open for school boards to make the curriculum content meet the needs and wishes of the local community.

It may seem like carrying coals to Newcastle to argue that the public schools can teach religion for, as a matter of fact, many states are already doing so, even some states where the anti-sectarian restrictions are the most rigid and where the public schools are the most completely secularized. It is a matter of common knowledge that chaplains from the various denominations are maintained at government expense in the army, in the navy, in the air corps, and in schools for all branches of our national Department of Defense. Chaplains, paid by the federal or state governments, are appointed to serve in both houses of the national Congress and of the several state legislatures, in penitentiaries, reform schools, mental hospitals, soldiers' homes, etc., but it may not be so well known that in orphanages, industrial schools, and schools under state Departments of Public Welfare, formal religious instruction is being carried on in one form or another.

Such instruction is conducted on the theory that, when children are separated from their parents by death or by court action, the state is under obligation to assume the religious responsibilities of the home, thus acting in place of the parents. In this way the states acknowledge their responsibility to teach religion to children who are deprived of parental guidance and of direct instruction by the church. Religious instruction under one plan or another is given by the states in such institutions in at least the following states: Maryland, North Carolina, Pennsylvania, Virginia, Colorado, Connecticut, Georgia, Idaho, Illinois, Massachusetts, Minnesota, Montana, and New Jersey. In some cases this instruction is given by the regular teachers in the school, in other cases by special teachers brought in for that purpose, and in still other cases by sending the children out to the churches for instruction. The particular method is by no means so important as is the obvious fact that in these special cases the state acknowledges its obligation to teach religion.

Now, if the state has an admitted responsibility for the religious instruction of children who are deprived of parental guidance, why should not that same principle lead it to acknowledge a similar obligation toward the children of parents who are delinquent in fulfilling the religious functions which the state expects them to discharge toward their children? Does not the state owe a very special obligation to the 50% or more of our public-school population who are not receiving religious training from any church and who, inferentially, are not receiving such guidance at home? Such an additional obligation would seem to be in line with the state's admitted responsibility for the religious training of children in its homes and institutions and in schools operated directly under state supervision and control. And there is no apparent way of reaching these millions of religiously illiterate boys and girls except through the public schools, especially since the Supreme Court of the United States has estopped the plans of the churches to bridge the gap. What the churches are prohibited from doing makes the responsibility of the schools all the more clear.

As Prof. George A. Coe has pointed out,[3] there is a thoroughly democratic process by which religion may find its place in the curriculum of the public schools. It is the way of discussion, of talking things over in small groups, in parent-teacher associations, in public mass meetings, in presentations from the pulpit, and, in

[3] See Chapter VI, page 68.

the end, by petitions brought before the school board and signed by a representative number of influential citizens. There are hundreds of religiously homogeneous communities, all over the country, where such an educational experiment would be welcomed if only an awareness of the situation were created.

It has been feared by many that the introduction of religion into our public schools would tend to awaken sectarian consciousness and foster sectarian prejudices, thus undermining the spirit of unity so essential to all democratic institutions. On the contrary, a frank facing of the existence of different religious groups of which the community is made up, and an emphasis on their basic agreements rather than upon their differences, would be the best possible way of dissipating the unintelligent sectarian prejudices already existing in the minds of school pupils. In commenting upon his proposed plan for theological schools to be maintained by the denominations on the campus of the University of Virginia, Thomas Jefferson said: "The want of instruction in the various creeds of religious faith existing among our citizens presents, therefore, a chasm in the general institution of the useful sciences. . . . By bringing the sects together, and mixing them with mass of other students, we shall soften their asperities, liberalize and neutralize their prejudices, and make the general religion a religion of peace, reason, and morality." [4] There is obvious soundness in Jefferson's conviction that sympathetic understanding will tend to allay prejudices, and this tendency will operate as potently in the elementary grades of education as upon the university level.

It has been argued in Chapter VII that religion is an essential element in general culture and that it is impossible to understand the history of any people without knowing something of the religious background of its development. It is also obvious that, to erase all references to religion and religious precepts from our public-school courses and textbooks in history, literature, music,

[4] 12 Ford, "Works of Jefferson, 272.

art and other similar cultural studies, would leave these courses and textbooks stripped of their vital meaning. This same statement may be said to apply also in the field of professional study. Joseph C. Duggan, former Assistant Attorney General of the United States, and also Assistant United States Attorney for the District of Massachusetts, has this to say with regard to the U.S. Supreme Court decision in the Champaign case: "It would be not only difficult, but impossible to teach law in any state university law school without transgressing the law of the Court, unless no mention was made of the religious, ecclesiastical, and moral precepts which constitute the foundation stones of such broad legal areas as equity, jurisprudence, and domestic relations. Similarly, the decision would rule out the teaching of courses in Religious History and Comparative Religion in all state-supported schools, especially where such courses are conducted by clergymen of any faith." [5] It should also be said that our understanding of the history of the ancient nations of the east would be much more meager were it not for connections and corroborations afforded by the Old Testament, and that any understanding of the history of Europe in the last two thousand years would be impossible without an acquaintance with the religious movements which are woven into its pages.

It is with a thrill of genuine refreshment that one reads the supplementary opinion filed by Mr. Justice Jackson in the Supreme Court record of the Champaign case, words which will long be remembered: "While we may and should end such formal and explicit instruction as the Champaign plan, and can at all times prohibit teaching of creed and ceremonial and can forbid forthright proselyting in the schools, I think it remains to be demonstrated whether it is possible, even if desirable, to comply with such demands as plaintiff's completely to isolate and cast out of secular education all that some people may reasonably regard

[5] "Religious Teaching in Public Schools," reprinted from *The Boston Pilot* of March 27, April 3 and 10, 1948.

as religious instruction. Perhaps such subjects as mathematics, physics, or chemistry are, or can be, completely secularized. But it would not seem practicable to teach either practice or appreciation of the arts if we are to forbid exposure of youth to any religious influence. Music without sacred music, architecture minus the cathedral, or painting without the scriptural themes would be eccentric and incomplete, even from a secular point of view. Yet the inspirational appeal of religion in these guises is often stronger than in forthright sermon. Even such a science as biology raises the issue between evolution and creation as an explanation of our presence on this planet. Certainly a course in English literature that omitted the Bible and other powerful uses of our mother tongue for religious ends would be pretty barren. And I would suppose it is a proper, if not an indispensable, part of preparation for a worldly life to know the roles that religion and religions have played in the tragic story of mankind. The fact is that, for good or ill, nearly everything in our culture worth transmitting, everything which gives meaning to life, is saturated with religious influences, derived from Paganism, Judaism, Christianity—both Protestant and Catholic—and other faiths accepted by a large part of the world's peoples. One can hardly respect a system of education that would leave the student wholly ignorant of the currents of religious thought that move the world society for a part in which he is being prepared."

Conclusion

Our forefathers laid deep and well the foundations of America's democratic public educational system. With prophetic insight they laid great stress upon the wide diffusion of elementary education and on what were known as the "three R's"—readin', 'ritin', and 'rithmetic—as the tools or instruments of all further culture. But underneath these "three R's" was another and greater R— *Religion*, which they laid down as the solid foundation on which the whole educational structure was to rest. When we recall the religious motivations which underlay our earlier education and made it effective in the production of rugged and dependable citizens, it is high time that we should "look into the rock whence we were hewn" and restore to religion its rightful and essential place in public education, ever remembering that "the fear of the Lord is the beginning of wisdom."

BIBLIOGRAPHY

Sources of General Information

Books

J. Paul Williams: THE NEW EDUCATION AND RELIGION (1945)
J. S. Brubacher *et al.*: THE PUBLIC SCHOOLS AND SPIRITUAL VALUES
W. S. Fleming: GOD IN OUR PUBLIC SCHOOLS (1942)
Samuel Windsor Brown: THE SECULARIZATION OF AMERICAN EDUCA-
TION
Raymond S. Culver: HORACE MANN AND RELIGION IN MASSACHUSETTS
PUBLIC SCHOOLS
W. W. Sweet: RELIGION IN COLONIAL AMERICA (1942)
Philip Schaff: CHURCH AND STATE
Alvin W. Johnson: CHURCH AND STATE RELATIONS IN THE UNITED
STATES
Conrad A. Hauser: TEACHING RELIGION IN THE PUBLIC SCHOOL (1942)
Paul Hutchinson: THE NEW LEVIATHAN (1946)
Joseph S. Clark: HISTORICAL SKETCH OF CONGREGATIONAL CHURCHES
IN MASSACHUSETTS FROM 1620 TO 1858
David Kemper Watson: THE CONSTITUTION OF THE UNITED STATES,
ITS HISTORY, APPLICATION, AND CONSTRUCTION (2 volumes,
1910)
Samuel E. Forman: LIFE AND WRITINGS OF THOMAS JEFFERSON
Virgil Henry: THE PLACE OF RELIGION IN THE PUBLIC SCHOOLS (1949)

Reports, Magazines, Periodicals, Etc.

RELIGION AND THE STATE, 1949 winter number of *Law and Contempo-
rary Problems*, issued by Duke University School of Law.
THE STATUS OF RELIGIOUS EDUCATION IN THE PUBLIC SCHOOLS, a sur-
vey prepared by the Research Division of the NEA and pub-
lished in 1949.
RELIGIOUS TEACHING IN THE PUBLIC SCHOOLS by Joseph C. Duggan,
of Boston College Law School. A comment on the U. S. Supreme
Court decision in the Champaign case. Reprinted from *The
Boston Pilot* of March 23 and April 3 and 19, 1948.
ILLINOIS SUPREME COURT OPINION No. 29678 in the case of The
People *ex rel.* Vashti McCollum (the Champaign case).

U. S. SUPREME COURT DECISION IN THE "NEW JERSEY BUS CASE," Everson *v.* Board of Education of the Township of Ewing, *et al.* Decision rendered February 10, 1947.

U. S. SUPREME COURT DECISION in the appeal of Mrs. Vashti McCollum from the decision of the Supreme Court of Illinois. Opinion rendered March 8, 1948.

A CRITICAL ANALYSIS OF THE U. S. SUPREME COURT DECISION in the Champaign case. Three articles in the *Christian Century* by Charles Clayton Morrison in the successive issues of June 8th, 15th, and 22nd, 1949.

MORAL AND SPIRITUAL VALUES IN EDUCATION, School Publication No. 402 of Los Angeles City Schools (1944–1945).

THE STATE AND SECTARIAN EDUCATION, NEA Research Bulletin, Vol. XXIV, No. 1, Feb. 1946.

SCHOOL EXPERIENCES WITH RELIGIOUS SIGNIFICANCE by Ernest J. Chave.

VARIOUS PROPOSALS FOR TEACHING RELIGION IN THE PUBLIC SCHOOLS, a Bulletin by Frank M. McKibben.

RELIGION AND PUBLIC EDUCATION, a conference report published by the American Council on Education Studies (1945).

THE RELATION OF RELIGION TO PUBLIC EDUCATION, the report of a special committee of the American Council on Education (1947).

OUR EDUCATIONAL DILEMMA, an article by W. W. Sweet in the *International Journal of Religious Education* (November, 1940).

ADEQUATE RELIGIOUS EDUCATION IN A FREE SOCIETY by J. Paul Williams, in *Religious Education,* January–February, 1946.

PROTESTANTISM AND THE PUBLIC SCHOOL by Charles Clayton Morrison in *The Christian Century,* April 17, 1946.

SHOULD RELIGION HAVE A DEFINITE PLACE IN THE PUBLIC SCHOOL CURRICULUM? by Herbert B. Mulford. Prepared for use in classes in administration and foundations of education in Northwestern University (February, 1947).

WHAT SORT OF RELIGION? by George Albert Coe in *The International Journal of Religious Education* (November, 1940).

ARE WEEKDAY CHURCH SCHOOLS THE SOLUTION? by Harrison S. Elliott in *The International Journal of Religious Education* (November, 1940).

TOTAL WAR AND THE CHRISTIAN CONSCIENCE by Martin H. Bickham in *Character and Citizenship* (September, 1945).

CHRISTIAN EDUCATION TODAY, a statement of basic philosophy published by The International Council of Religious Education (1940).

RELATION OF RELIGION TO PUBLIC EDUCATION by Ordway Tead, *Hazen Pamphlets* (1944).

WEEKDAY CLASSES IN RELIGION by Mary Dabney Davis. Bulletin No. 3, U. S. Office of Education (1941).

RELIGION AND PUBLIC EDUCATION by F. Ernest Johnson in *Information Service* (January 2, 1943).

ONE WORLD FOR RELIGION, TOO by Harry Emerson Fosdick. An address before the Protestant Council of the City of New York, briefed in *The Reader's Digest* for May, 1946.

Sources of Statistical Information

Statistics on the Crime Situation in the United States

FEDERAL BUREAU OF INVESTIGATION
Annual Report for 1944.
Semi-Annual Bulletin No. 1 for 1945.
Annual Bulletin for 1945.
Semi-Annual Bulletin No. 1, 1946.
Semi-Annual Bulletin No. 1, 1947.
"Crime and Juvenile Delinquency"—Bulletin of July 14, 1947.
Also numerous other bulletins and mimeographed reports sent by Mr. J. Edgar Hoover from time to time, as follows:
"Youth Running Wild"—Reprinted from *This Week Magazine* (1943).
"Crime Challenges the Churches"—November 29, 1944.
"The Golden Rule—Against Juvenile Crime"—Reprinted from *The Civetan Magazine*, August, 1945.
"There Will Be a Postwar Crime Wave Unless"—Reprinted from *The Rotarian Magazine*, April, 1945.
"The Juvenile Delinquency Problem"—*FBI Bulletin* of April, 1945.
Radio Interview with Richard Harkness, February 13, 1946.
"The Country's Opportunity"—Reprinted from *The Leatherneck*, January, 1946.
"The Reconversion of Law Enforcement," an address at the 52nd annual meeting of Chiefs of Police at Miami, Florida, December 19, 1945.

Address to Catholic Youth Organization, January 8, 1946.
"Crime Begins at Home"—Reprinted from the *Redbook Magazine*, October, 1946.
"How Good a Parent Are You?"—Reprinted from *This Week Magazine*, April 20, 1947.

Sources of General Statistical Information

Records of personal studies in Sunday School statistics covering a period of forty years.

"Marriage and Divorce in the U. S. from 1937 to 1945"—A special report of the U. S. Bureau of Vital Statistics, September 10, 1946.

"Historical Summary of Education," 1941–1942, Vol. II, Chap. II, U. S. Office of Education.

"Statistics of Non-Public Elementary and Secondary Schools," 1940–1941, Vol. II, Chap. IX, U. S. Office of Education.

"U. S. Census of Religious Bodies," 1906, 1916, 1926, 1936.

U. S. Annual reports of population from 1870 to 1947, inclusive.

Official Sunday School Statistics of the Methodist Church from 1845 to 1947, inclusive. (Prior to 1939 the record was for the Methodist Episcopal Church only.)

Special statistical reports of The International Council of Religious Education, of the Yearbook of the Churches, and of *The Christian Herald*.

"Historical Sketch of Congregational Churches in Massachusetts from 1620 to 1858" by Joseph S. Clark.

APPENDIX

Sects and Number of Churches in Massachuetts

Sect	Churches	Sect	Churches
1800		*1936 Cont.*	
Congregationalist	344	Advent Christian	28
Baptist	93	Greek Orthodox	25
Methodist	29	Presbyterian (U.S.A.)	24
Episcopal	14	Nazarene	23
Quaker	8	Scandinavian Evang.	22
Universalist	4	Lutheran (Missouri Syn)	19
Presbyterian	2	African Methodist	17
Roman Catholic	1	Assemblies of God	17
		Plymouth Brethren	16
1858		Friends	14
Orthodox Cong.	490	National Spiritualist As.	13
Meth. Episcopal	277	New Jerusalem	12
Baptist	266	Primitive Methodist	11
Unitarian	170	Independent	10
Universalist	135	Christodelphians	10
Episcopalian	65	Albanian Orthodox	9
Roman Catholic	64	Latter Day Saints (Reorg.)	9
Christian	37	African Meth. Epis. Zion	9
Friends Meetings	24	Polish National Catholic	9
Free Will Baptist	21	United Presbyterian	8
Methodist Protestant	20	Finnish Evangelical Luth.	8
Second Adventist	15	Christian & Missionary All.	7
Wesleyan Methodist	13	Church of Armenia	7
Swedenborgian	11	Russian Orthodox	7
Presbyterian	7	Evangelical	7
Shaker	4	United Lutheran	6
Unclassified	12	Church of God	5
		Church of God & Saints of Christ	5
1936		Disciples of Christ	5
Roman Catholic	708	Syrian Antiochian Orthodox	5
Congregational	557	Latter Day Saints	5
Methodist Episcopal	294	National Spiritual All.	5
Northern Baptist	272	Bahais	4
Protestant Episcopal	264	Church of God in Christ	4
Jewish	186	Volunteers of America	4
Unitarian	140	Plymouth Brethren I	3
Christian Science	79	Plymouth Brethren IV	3
Universalist	70	Finnish Evang. Nat. Luth.	3
Federated	52	Free Methodist	3
Salvation Army	46	N. America Old Roman Cath.	3
Negro Baptist	39	International Pentecost	3
Lutheran (Augustana)	36	United Holy Church	3
Seventh Adventist	33	All other denominations	40

Present Status of Bible Reading in the Public Schools [1]

The Bible is now read devotionally every day in the public schools of about 40 million Americans—nearly a third of our entire population —mainly quite a recent return to the old custom. Twelve states by mandatory law read a portion of Scripture every day in every school room. The states, with the dates of the passage of the law, are as follows:

Massachusetts	1855	Maine	1923
Pennsylvania	1913	Delaware	1923
Tennessee	1915	Kentucky	1924
New Jersey	1916	Florida	1925
Alabama	1919	Idaho	1925
Georgia	1921	Arkansas	1930

Many large cities outside of these states, headed by New York, Baltimore, Washington, D. C., by school Board rule use the Bible devotionally in all school rooms. Our latest investigation about three years ago (about 1939) revealed 38 cities of over 100,000 population (almost half of such cities in the United States) use the Bible with religious intent in all rooms. . . . In addition to the above twelve states, 8 others by law forbid the exclusion of the Bible from their schools—Iowa, Indiana, the two Dakotas, Kansas, Oklahoma, Mississippi, New York, the latter applying to the metropolis only. Thus twenty states by definite law require the daily use of the Bible in their schools or specifically forbid its exclusion therefrom.

Six other states have decisions from their highest courts giving the book complete right of way in the public schools—Ohio, Michigan, Minnesota, Nebraska, Colorado and Texas. According to this count, so far there are 26 states that either by direct statute or Supreme Court decision open schoolhouse doors to the Book of God. The Supreme Courts of Illinois and Washington shut schoolhouse doors against the Bible. The high courts of Wisconsin and Louisiana give split decisions, partly closing the doors to the Book. The South Dakota Court argues against the Bible in the schools but leaves it there. There is considerable uncertainty, but it seems that, by interpretation, attorneys general or state superintendents exclude the Bible from the schools of 6 states: California, Nevada, Arizona, Wyoming, Utah and New York. We find

[1] From "God In Our Public Schools," W. S. Fleming, pages 1943–5.

no law, court decision or official interpretation that interferes with the use of the Bible in the remaining states: Vermont, New Hampshire, Connecticut, Rhode Island, Maryland, West Virginia, North Carolina, South Carolina, Missouri and Oregon. In some states correspondence shows the Bible in large use in the schools; in others little attention is given to the religious note.

Dates of Adoption of Anti-Sectarian Laws by the Several States

States Amending Constitutions		*States Adopting Provision When Admitted to the Union*	
New Jersey	1844	Wisconsin	1848
Michigan	1850	Oregon	1857
Ohio	1851	Kansas	1859
Indiana	1851	Nevada	1864
Massachusetts	1855	Nebraska	1867
Iowa	1857	West Virginia	1872
Mississippi	1868	Colorado	1876
South Carolina	1868	North Dakota	1889
Arkansas	1868	South Dakota	1889
Illinois	1870	Montana	1889
Pennsylvania	1872	Washington	1889
Alabama	1875	Idaho	1890
Missouri	1875	Wyoming	1890
North Carolina	1876	Utah	1896
Texas	1876	Oklahoma	1907
Minnesota	1877	New Mexico	1912
Georgia	1877	Arizona	1912
California	1879		
Louisiana	1879		
Florida	1885		
Delaware	1897		

What the Teachers Think [2]

On June 23, 1941, the Chicago Teachers' Union stated their educational platform as follows:

1. The Chicago Teachers' Union believes that social attitudes, character training, and training for citizenship are major objectives of public

[2] From *Chicago Union Teacher*, April, 1948.

school education, and points out that they have been so regarded by educational authorities for many years.

2. The Chicago Teachers' Union recommends renewed effort upon and evaluation of the public school program on character education, citizenship training, and social attitudes and reminds Chicago citizens that the Chicago Teachers' Union has continuously fought for policies consistent with this recommendation.

3. The Chicago Teachers' Union appreciates the efforts that have long been made by the religious agencies of Chicago—efforts in which many of its members participated—toward a higher spiritual life for our young people, and hopes that these efforts will continue and be extended.

4. The Chicago Teachers' Union believes that any official connection of the public schools with religious agencies in a program of religious education is in effect a violation of the fundamental American principle of the separation of church and state, and is thus unwise. The Union is therefore opposed to the forming or maintaining of any such connection.

At the 1946 convention of the American Federation of Teachers, the teachers' union took a similar stand nationally, this action is to be found on page 17 of the November, 1946, issue of the *American Teacher Magazine*.

Author's note—The fourth paragraph of the above statement of principles antedates by seven years the U. S. Supreme Court decision on the Champaign case. In noting that fact, one should not fail to notice that not only the Chicago teachers but also the national organization have in strong language put themselves on record as favoring the fullest possible extension of the elements of training that make for character development and social usefulness. Such a platform is a great credit to the rank and file of America's teachers.